FROM
PRAIRIE KITCHENS

FROM
PRAIRIE KITCHENS

Recipes by
Saskatchewan Women's Institute

Compiled by EMMIE ODDIE

Western Producer Prairie Books
Saskatoon, Saskatchewan

Copyright © 1980 compiled by
The Saskatchewan Women's Institute
Western Producer Prairie Books
Saskatoon, Saskatchewan
Third printing 1981

Jacket and book design by Mac Thorpe
Cover photo by F:11 Photographic Design Ltd., Commercial Division
Photographer — Stirling Ward
Printed and bound in Canada by Modern Press
Saskatoon, Saskatchewan

Western Producer Prairie Books publications are
produced and manufactured in the middle of
western Canada by a unique publishing venture
owned by a group of prairie farmers who are
members of Saskatchewan Wheat Pool. Our first
book in 1954 was a reprint of a serial originally
carried in *The Western Producer*, a weekly
newspaper serving western Canadian farmers
since 1923. We continue the tradition of providing
enjoyable and informative reading for all
Canadians.

CANADIAN CATALOGUING IN PUBLICATION DATA

Oddie, Emmie 1916-
     From prairie kitchens
     Includes index
     ISBN 0-88833-011-1

     1. Cookery   I. Women's Institutes of
Saskatchewan II. Title
TX715.O33 641.5 C80-091027-3

TABLE OF CONTENTS

PREFACE

Every branch of the Saskatchewan Women's Institute, whether large or small, had a hand in creating this book. "Project cookbook" was born in 1975 when interim committee members came together over coffee at a restaurant near Grenfell, Saskatchewan. Their idea was subsequently accepted at a provincial convention, and a committee was struck with Merle Williamson to act as chairperson and to provide liaison with the SWI Board, Lil McCutcheon to investigate grants or other financial assistance, Ada Nelson to scout out printing services, and Emmie Oddie to oversee collection of the recipes.

Each branch was eligible to contribute one recipe in each of seven categories: casserole, ethnic, pioneer, festive, low calorie/low joule, whole grain and outdoor. Each branch chose its own method of reaching a decision about the recipes to be submitted. Some, like the Tregarva group, had fun bringing together a gamut of dishes to taste and judge: the distinguished tortiére beat the perogies and the apricot pie in the ethnic class and later won a place in the book. After the final selection, the recipes were rewritten using a standard format.

The preliminary selection of the recipes brought the "cookbook lieutenants" into the act. They were M. Williamson of Rocanville who was responsible for ethnic dishes; Ivy McVicar of Prairie River (outdoor recipes), Mrs. J. E. Armitage of Redvers and Mrs. H. J. Madsen of Wauchope (pioneer cookery), Judi McDonald of Rosetown (natural foods), Emmie Oddie of Tregarva (low-calorie recipes), and Alison Wilson of Glenbain (festive foods). Each lieutenant sorted and edited the recipes in a specific category, culled duplicates, and sent the collection to SWI branches in her district for testing. At the same time, she distributed check lists and evaluation sheets for use by the three different homemakers who would test each recipe. Outdoor recipes, for example, were assigned to the SWI branches in northeastern Saskatchewan; their members had to hurry to complete testing before the first bleak fall weather.

When testing and evaluation were completed, the recipes were returned to the lieutenants for another culling and sorting, then back to the branches for a final check.

In the meantime the lieutenants had been practising with metric measures in preparation for the next phase. Emmie Oddie, the recipe captain, had put together instructions for adapting recipes to metric, and the branches acquired the appropriate measures and went at the job (some a bit reluctantly). The lieutenants then funnelled their collections back to the captain and the Tregarva WI who checked the metric conversions. Special recognition should go to the "cookbook lieutenants"; to Margaret Pattilo, Jean Renault, Elma Schultz, Ada

Nelson, Lillian McCutcheon; to Kathy Groshong for the name "From Prairie Kitchens"; and to Ruth and Grace Busby, Eunice Jorgensen, Sandra Stephenson, Nina Grudnizski, Colleen Dickson and Lynn Pearce of the Tregarva WI branch for the work they did tasting, testing and making corrections. In some recipes, proportions were not too important but in others they were crucial and experienced cooks applied common sense.

The Women's Institute of Saskatchewan has a great reputation, surely in part due to the culinary achievements of the membership. We are pleased to share our kitchen successes with you. We hope you will also enjoy reading about our history and our other accomplishments.

The Women's Institute of Saskatchewan or Homemakers' Clubs as they were first named, were organized in 1911. Before that time there had been a number of women's clubs functioning independently under different names but with similar objectives — to improve rural communities and to bring women together for social and mental stimulation. During the autumn of 1910, Miss Lillian Beynon (later Mrs. A. V. Thomas of Winnipeg), was hired by the Extension Division of the University of Saskatchewan to help organize new clubs along the lines of the Women's Institutes in Ontario.

In January, 1911, women's groups were invited to send delegates to a convention in Regina. As a result of these meetings, the Homemakers' Clubs of Saskatchewan came into being, under the motto "From Home and Country."

During the early years, the clubs were administered as a branch of the Extension Division of the university. As the work load grew, it was found necessary to place the supervision of the women's groups in the hands of a qualified director. In 1913, Miss Abigail DeLury was appointed director of women's work, a position she held until July, 1930. Under her capable and sympathetic supervision, the organization grew steadily. Miss Bertha Oxner, who succeeded Miss DeLury, provided 19 years of energetic and inspiring direction to the clubs. She was later made the first Honorary Life Member of the Homemakers' Clubs. Miss Alice Stevens, who succeeded Miss Oxner and made a lasting and appreciated contribution, resigned in 1952, shortly before her death. Miss Margaret Pattillo is now responsible for carrying on the traditional contributions of the Extension Division of the University of Saskatchewan to the Women's Institutes. Under her, the interests of the branches have widened, and a new spirit of independence has been fostered.

Homemakers served well during the two World Wars by aiding the Red Cross in its work at the front and in Canada. During the years of drought and depression, determination and ingenuity were demonstrated as well. Homemakers' Clubs provided stimulation for many communities at that difficult time. An increase in the number of clubs in the northern part of the province, greater co-operation with other institutions working for community betterment, and encouragement of projects for girls and young women were characteristic of that period.

Since their inception, Homemakers' Clubs have been community-minded. As nonpartisan and nonsectarian groups, they have welcomed women of all religious faiths and from many racial backgrounds. Newcomers who spoke little English found that their demonstrations of old-country cookery and handicrafts formed a bridge which quickly led to understanding.

A plaque unveiled on the campus of the University of Saskatchewan in 1976 recognized the contribution made by Homemakers' Clubs — Women's Institutes.

"Rural life has been marked by solitude. The Homemakers' Clubs have worked to increase communications among farm women and to improve the rural community, since their formation in 1911 by the University of Saskatchewan's Extension Services. Local meetings provided a place for all women to meet and learn new homemaking skills. Rural communities benefited from local clubs' sponsorship of music and drama festivals, libraries and community halls. These clubs helped to create an awareness of the need for social reform. While avoiding politics, they pressured governments to improve grid roads, rural health and educational services and to change laws which adversely affected women. After 1972 the clubs continued to work for a better rural life, under the name of Women's Institutes."

In 1975-76 (International Women's Year), leadership-development workshops were held for SWI members in various parts of Saskatchewan. The purpose was to make participants more effective spokesmen for and on behalf of rural women. Since 1972, SWI has provided small bursaries to help members attend courses of their own choice. Learning about spinning and weaving was the preference of one member who later wrote a booklet about natural dyes made from plants and plant materials indigenous to the area.

The Institutes also encourage achievement and excellence through provincial, national, and international competitions. At the provincial level, for example, there is the J & P Coats contest for needlecraft. Besides workmanship, original design is an important factor considered in the judging. Saskatchewan needlewomen have gone on to win in the national Tweedsmuir Competition, and in 1979, Euphie Thomson of Pense advanced to take second place in the international level competition with her contemporary wallhanging. Similar success stories could be told about the achievements of SWI members in writing and visual arts contests.

SWI has also contributed to the education of its members through the *Second Penny*, a newspaper which goes to each member, and the "Brown Envelope", which is mailed out to the branches from the

SWI office in Saskatoon. Much valuable and thought-provoking information is passed along through these channels.

A highly successful experiment in "learning by doing" was the travel exchange between New Brunswick and Saskatchewan WIs. In 1975 New Brunswick women came west, and the next year 40 fortunate Saskatchewanians travelled east. An unforgettable experience for all concerned!

In the belief that much benefit can result from co-operation with like-minded groups, the SWI maintains affiliations with the Federated Women's Institute of Canada and with the Associated Country Women of the World, an international group with members in 66 countries. Other affiliations are with the Saskatchewan Federation of Agriculture, the Saskatchewan Council of Women, the Consumers' Association of Canada, the Saskatchewan Safety Council, the Saskatchewan Association of Human Rights, the Saskatchewan Action Committee on the Status of Women, and the United Nations Association.

SWI members are rightly proud of their "Sewing Machine Project." Between 1965 and 1975, they contributed over 300 sewing machines and 270 kits of sewing supplies to Indian women who had acquired certain sewing skills. No one will ever know how many 4-H clubs have been helped by SWI or how many Institute members have acted as 4-H leaders, supported local fairs and music festivals, and tended cemeteries. Countless scholarships, bursaries, trophies, and prizes have been given by SWI branches to young people in their communities. For example, each year the Institute donates the SWI Prize and the Bertha Oxner Scholarship for students entering second and third-year home economics at the University of Saskatchewan.

The continuing education of its own members has also been a focus of the SWI's work. In order to give guidance to clubs in planning their programs, standing committees have been organized on agriculture and Canadian industry, arts and literature, education, home economics, international relations, legislation, and public health. These committees have conveners in the individual branches as well as at the district and provincial levels.

There are 25 districts in the Saskatchewan Women's Institute. The branches within these districts are listed below:

Regina-Moose Jaw District: Dundee, Eastview, Francis, Grand Coulee, Pense, Tregarva, Tyvan. *Yorkton District*: Ashdown, Briarmound, Creekside, Tuffnell. *Lashburn District*: Bresaylor, Frenchman Butte, Furness, Hearthside, Northern Circle, Paynton, South Lashburn. *Davidson District*: Aylesbury, Bladworth, Chatham, Craik, Hanley. *Govan District*: Crosswoods, Dysart, Lakeshore, Nokomis, Prairie Rose, Punnichy, Simpson, Usborne, Venn. *Robinhood District*: Idylwild, Livelong, Robinhood, West Hazel. *Hawarden District*: Bounty, Glenside, Hawarden. *Quill Plains District*: Caledon, Clair, Kylemore, Quill Lake, Westport. *The Battlefords District*: Glenrose,

Highgate, Maymont, Meadow Lake, Meota, Mount Hope, Prince, Prongua, Radisson, Richard, Ruddell, Whitewood Lake. *Swarthmore District*: Abbeywood, Cut Knife, Dufferin, Rosebrier, Rosemary, Unity, Wasteena, Weewona, Westside, Wilbert. *Kindersley District*: Antelope Park, Dewar Lake, Englewood, Marengo, Merid, Merrington, Pinkham. *Blackley District*: Bradwell, Cory Busy Bees, Delisle, Environ, Hawoods, Patience Lake, Pike Lake, Zelma. *Soo Line District*: Abbott, Ceylon, Glenwood, Greenville, Halbrite, Hitchcock, Kingsford, North Weyburn, South Weyburn, Torquay, Trossachs, West Weyburn, Yellow Grass. *Prince Albert District*: Canwood, Colleston, Marcelin, Paddockwood, Uranium City, Wild Rose. *Swift Current District*: Burnham, Pambrun, Sceptre, Success, Swift Current, Val Marie. *Nipawin District*: Glen Horne, Glocca Morra, Moose Plains. *Gull Lake District*: Bear Creek, Golden Sheaf, Lloyd, Lowell, Robsart, Valley Centre. *Pipestone Valley District*: Buffalo Plains, Corning, Grenfell, Handsworth, Inchkeith, Langbank, Mount Murray, Stonybrook, Summerhill. *Carrot River Valley District*: Golburn Valley, Leather River, Maple Leaf, Resource, Melfort View, Salopian. *Beechy District*: Beechy, Buffalo Basin, Suncrest. *Carlyle Lake District*: Bellhouse-Parkman, Carnduff, Excelsior, Fertile, Glen Adelaide, Manor, Maryfield. *Maria Kilden District*: Prairie River, Spruceville, Three-Rivers. *Elrose District*: Camberley, Glamis, Hughton, Plato. *Greater Prosperity District*: Carnoustie, Dubuc, E.U.K., Gerald, North Log, Prosperity, Welwyn. *Assiniboia District*: Glen Bain, Kelstern, Mazenod, Melaval, Winnabel. *Ogema District*: Harptree, Glasnevan, Hatty Valley.

The Saskatchewan Women's Institute is proud of its history and proud too of the effort which has gone into this cookbook. The recipes in this collection reflect life as WI members live it, some struggling with low-calorie diets, some devoted to granola and all taking pride in the gourmet offerings they donate to pot-luck and fowl suppers or serve at family or wedding feasts. Saskatchewan is wealthy in the diversity of her nationalities. The ethnic recipes come from our own people. What's more, we are a great wheat-producing province and proud of it. Our cooks are aware, too, of their prowess in baking.

We hope that these recipes will bring an aspect of Saskatchewan life into kitchens everywhere.

Emmie Oddie
Cookbook Captain
Regina, Sask.
Elma Schultz
Watson, Saskatchewan

METRIC IN THE KITCHEN

Bottles, cartloads and stones all have in common that at one time they were units of measurement. To this list soon will be added cups, tablespoons and teaspoons, terms which will become obsolete as the result of the federal government's adoption of the International System of Units (SI), commonly known as metric.

This cookbook has been prepared with all recipes in both Imperial and metric measures. Many homemakers will continue to use their present measuring equipment until it becomes lost or broken. Some cooks, with their new measuring equipment, can begin immediately using metric measures.

ABOUT MEASURING

The metric symbols which will frequently be used in the kitchen are in the chart below:

QUANTITY	NAME OF UNIT	SYMBOL
Temperature	degree Celsius	°C
Volume	litre (1000 mL)	L
	millilitre	mL
Mass	kilogram (1000 g)	kg
	gram	g
Length	metre (100 cm)	m
	centimetre (10 mm)	cm
	millimetre	mm
Energy	joule	J
Pressure	kilopascal	kPa

The well-stocked metric cupboard should hold these measures:
a) liquid - 250 mL, 500 mL, 1000 mL or 1 litre
b) dry - 50 mL, 125 mL, 250 mL (set of three)
c) small measures (set of five) - 1, 2, 5, 15, and 25 mL

A few recipes will involve units of weight. A kilogram (1000 grams) converts to slightly more than two pounds.

In Canadian kitchens metric cooking is easy because cooks retain volume measurement although they change to a new set of measures. Generally metric recipes will turn out to be about 5% larger because equivalents are rounded off to take advantage of a decimal system.

METRIC RECIPES IN THIS BOOK

The standard recipes that appear in this book were not converted to metric measures, but adapted, adjusted and then tested. Quantities as much as possible take advantage of the decimal system to ensure a minimum use of utensils. Therefore, do not expect precise uniformity in conversion. What appears is really a new recipe. At time of publication some pre-packaged ingredients have not been rounded and care has been taken to specify the metric size of containers now appearing on the grocery shelf. For example, the 10-ounce can is now 284 mL.

ADAPTING YOUR OWN RECIPES

The cup is replaced by the 250 mL measure, the half cup by 125 mL. Suppose your old recipe used ⅓ cup. Try to use a combination of the new measures (50 + 25) to make 75 mL which is not very far out for the exact numerical division 250/3.

The following benchmarks will be useful for beginners:

250 mL replaces an 8 ounce cup
 15 mL replaces one tablespoon
  5 mL replaces one teaspoon
  5 cm about 2 inches
  1 kg a little more than 2 pounds
500 g is a little more than 1 pound
100°C water boils
160°C oven temperature for roasting

OVEN TEMPERATURE REPLACEMENTS

Familiar Fahrenheit appliance temperatures will be replaced by the Celsius temperatures below:

100°C	200°F
110°C	225°F
120°C	250°F
140°C	275°F
150°C*	300°F
160°C*	325°F
180°C*	350°F
190°C*	375°F
200°C*	400°F
220°C*	425°F
230°C*	450°F
240°C	475°F
260°C	500°F

* most commonly used temperatures.

BAKEWARE

New baking dishes will be measured in centimeters. A centimeter is slightly less than half an inch. Counterparts of faithful familiar pans:

Loaf:	9 x 5 x 3 inches = 22 cm x 12 cm x 7 cm
Round:	8 inch diameter = 20 cm x 4 cm
Tube:	9 inch = 22 cm x 10 cm
Bundt:	10 inch = 25 cm
Pie Plate:	8 inch = 20 cm x 2.5 cm
	9 inch = 22.5 cm
	10 inch = 25 cm
Cake Pans:	8 x 8 x 3 inches = 10.0 cm x 5.0 cm
	9 x 9 x 2 inches = 22.0 cm x 5.0 cm
	15 x 10 x 2 inches = 37 cm x 25 cm x 5 cm

COOKING TEMPERATURES FOR MEAT

Oven temperatures set at 160°C (320°F)

VARIETY	DEGREE OF COOKING	INTERNAL TEMPERATURE	
		°C	°F
		(approximate)	
Beef	Rare	60°C	140°F
	Medium	65°C	150°F
	Well done	75°C	170°F
Veal	Well done	80°C	175°F
Lamb	Rare	60°C	140°F
	Medium	70°C	160°F
	Well done	75°C	170°F
Pork – cured	Ready to serve	55°C	130°F
	Cook and serve	70°C	160°F
	Picnic, etc.	75°C	170°F
Pork – fresh		80°C	175°F
Poultry- (in thigh)		85°C	185°F

BAKING TEMPERATURES

PRODUCT	OVEN TEMPERATURE		TIMES (Minutes)
	°F (approx) °C		
BREAD, etc.			
Cream puffs, popovers	375°F	190°C	60
Muffins	400-425°F	200-220°C	20-25
Quick Breads	350-375°F	180-190°C	60-75
Tea Biscuits	425-450°F	220-230°C	10-15
Yeast Bread	400°F	200°C	30-40
Yeast Rolls, plain	400°F	200°C	20-25
Yeast Rolls, sweet	375°F	190°C	20-30
CAKES WITHOUT FAT			
Angel and sponge (tube pan)	340-350°F	170-180°C	50-60
CAKES WITH FAT			
Cup	350-375°F	180-190°C	15-25
Layer	350-375°F	180-190°C	20-35
Square, rectangle	350°F	180°C	45-60
COOKIES			
Drop	350-400°F	180-200°C	8-15
Rolled	375°F	190°C	8-10
EGG, MEAT, MILK AND CHEESE DISHES			
Cheese souffle, custards (baked in a pan of hot water)	350°F	180°C	30-60
Macaroni and cheese	350°F	180°C	25-30
Meat Loaf	350°F	180°C	60-90
Meat Pie	400°F	200°C	25-30
Rice Pudding (raw rice)	300°F	150°C	120-180
Scalloped Potatoes	350°F	180°C	60
PASTRY			
One crust pie (unbaked shell)	400-425°F	200-220°C	30-40
Meringue on cooked filling in pre-baked shell	350-425°F	180-220°C	12-15
Shell only	450°F	230°C	10-12
Two crust pies with uncooked filling	400-425°F	200-220°C	45-55
Two crust pies with cooked filling	425-450°F	220-230°C	30-45

When baking in ovenproof glassware, reduce temperature 10°C (25°F). For example, when using a glass pie pan, bake at 220°C (425°F) instead of 230°C (450°F) given in chart.

TEMPERATURES FOR DEEP-FAT FRYING

PRODUCT	TEMPERATURE OF FAT		
	°F	(approx)	°C
Chicken	345°F		175°C
Doughnuts, fish, fritters	345-375°F		175-190°C
Croquettes, onions, eggplant	375-390°F		190-195°C
French Fried Potatoes	390-400°F		195-200°C

* At high altitudes, the lower boiling point of water in foods requires lowering of temperatures for deep-fat frying.

TEMPERATURES AND TESTS FOR SYRUP AND CANDIES

PRODUCT	TEMPERATURE OF SYRUP AT SEA LEVEL* (Indicating Concentration Desired)		TEST
	°F (approx)	°C	
Syrup	225-230°F	110-112°C	Thread
Fondant Fudge Panocha	230-240°F	112-115°C	Soft Ball
Caramels	245-250°F	118-120°C	Firm Ball
Divinity Marshmallows Popcorn Balls	250-265°F	121-130°C	Hard Ball
Butterscotch Taffies	270-290°F	132-143°C	Soft crack
Brittle Glace	300-310°F	149-154°C	Hard crack
Barley sugar	325°F	160°C	Clear liquid
Caramel	340°F	170°C	Brown liquid

* Cook the syrup about 1°C (2°F) lower than temperature at sea level for each increase of 300 m (or 280 m) (approx. 900-1000 feet) in elevation.

CASSEROLES

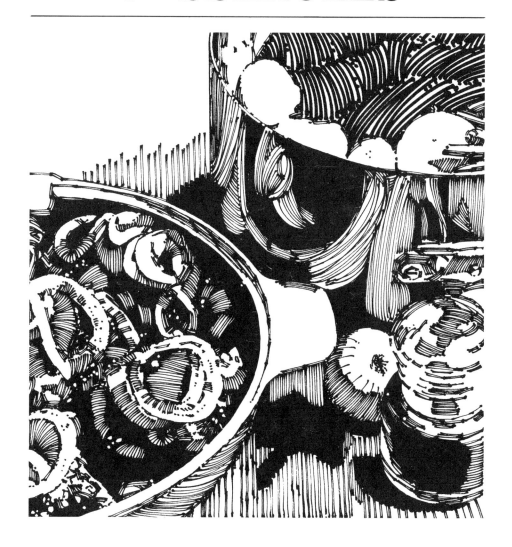

MAKING CASSEROLES is like magic. The reward of creating a delectable new dish which comes steaming from the oven is a pleasure every cook has experienced. But the chief appeal is convenience. Preparation and dish-washing may be whipped out of the way in the morning so that the cook may turn to other things while the dinner is heating. And the homemaker going off to garden or to help with chores around the farm can be assured that the one dish casserole will provide the family's nutritional needs at dinner.

The proliferation of organizations in rural centers have made increasing demands on the homemaker. This trend has enhanced the popularity of casseroles. Advance preparation permits active participation in community events without delaying scheduled meal times. It is a simple matter of returning home to pop a tempting casserole into the oven, or, if it is convenient, assigning this task to another member of the family. Another group of homemakers, those who have taken jobs outside the home, acknowledge that the casserole facilitates easy meal planning. Tripling a favorite recipe and freezing extra casseroles for busy days or entertaining is good time and energy management for anyone. And for those who consider thrift an important factor, casseroles offer an opportunity to use left-over food, adding economy to the enjoyment of preparation.

Casseroles have a special significance for prairie people, in part due to the large acreages so unique to western Canada. From pioneer days until the present, the two major farming events, seeding and harvesting, have necessitated a work day that begins at dawn and does not cease until sunset. As a result of the long distances separating the home and field, few operators have been able to afford the expenditure of time required to make the trip. It quickly became the practice for homemakers to journey to the field with prepared food, and no meal was more convenient or nutritious than the single dish casserole. For some, it is part of an enjoyable tradition to "picnic" in the field, substituting the tailgate of a truck or the back of a station wagon for a table top.

Most casseroles are made in the approximate proportions of one-third protein rich food, one-third pasta or starchy vegetable, and one-third white or brown sauce, soup or meat broth. To any basic combination the cook may add those touches that turn the dish into a real treat — pimiento strips, slices of green pepper, grated cheese, parsley, sliced olives or mushrooms.

Toppings on casseroles are not always necessary but can add flavor and appearance to the dish. Buttered cracker or bread crumbs, crumbled corn flakes, even a sprinkling of paprika or a few slivered nuts can dress up an otherwise ordinary casserole.

Saskatchewan Women's Institute members are anxious to share a few of the practical recipes they find useful to ease the work on very busy days.

HINTS FOR FREEZING CASSEROLES

Most casseroles of cooked or partially cooked ingredients freeze well. There are certain considerations:

1. Undercook the casseroles intended for the freezer. Additional cooking will take place during reheating.
2. Not all ingredients freeze equally well: Avoid
   (a) potatoes and hard cooked eggs which lose quality.
   (b) onions and herbs that change strength in freezing.
   (c) casseroles with high fat content as the fat tends to separate.
3. Homemade sauce made with wheat flour may separate somewhat during freezing. Commercial soups are sometimes made with rice flour which produces a smoother product.
4. Casserole toppings should be added prior to reheating.
5. To freeze casseroles, line the dish with heavy aluminum foil leaving long ends (enough to wrap around the food and seal over the top). Pour in the food and seal the foil with a double fold. Place casserole in freezer until food is frozen solid. Then remove the frozen food from the casserole for storage. Of course casseroles may be frozen in the baking dish if you have dishes to spare.
6. To reheat, remove foil and return the food to the original casserole dish. Either thaw in the refrigerator and cook as soon as thawed, or place the frozen casserole in the oven directly. If reheating the frozen item in the oven, allow additional time.
7. Do not use too large a dish for a frozen casserole because food may burn around the edge before it is warm in the center. Placing the casserole in a pan of water also helps to prevent burning. No single rule for time and temperature can apply to all casseroles as proportions vary greatly.
8. Do not refreeze the thawed casserole.
9. For top quality and good freezer management, frozen casseroles should be used up in about one month.

FISHERMAN'S FAVORITE

Don't forget the raisins, they are the surprise ingredient in this hearty soup; it is a one-dish meal.

1	ham bone	1
12	cups water	3 L
½	cup pot barley or rice	125 mL
1	medium onion, chopped	1
1	tablespoon salt	15 mL
½	teaspoon pepper	2 mL
6	slices bacon or 6 wieners	6
1	cup chopped celery	250 mL
4	medium potatoes, diced	4
2½	cups vegetables (peas, beans, carrots)	625 mL
½	cup raisins	125 mL
3	5-ounce cans baby clams or equivalent in fresh clams	426 g

Into large pot put ham bone, water, barley or rice, onion and seasonings. Simmer for at least 2 hours.

Fry bacon and cut in pieces or cut up wieners. One hour before soup is to be served, add bacon or wieners, celery, potatoes, vegetables and raisins. Just before serving, add clams and clam-liquor. Simmer until serving time. Yield: 12 servings.

TOP-OF-STOVE CHEESE SOUFFLÉ

You will need a double-boiler with 8-cup (2 L) top and tight-fitting lid.

1½	tablespoons butter or margarine	25 mL
2	tablespoons flour	30 mL
½	teaspoon dry mustard	2 mL
½	teaspoon salt	2 mL
¼	teaspoon pepper	1 mL
1	cup milk	250 mL
1	cup old cheddar cheese, grated	250 mL
4	eggs, separated	4

In a small sauce pan, melt butter, then add flour, mustard and seasonings. Add milk, stirring until thick. Remove from heat and stir in cheese until melted. In a large bowl, beat egg yolks until thick; then stir into sauce slowly. In another bowl, beat egg whites until they form soft (not stiff) peaks; gently fold whites into cheese sauce.

Pour into the ungreased top of the double boiler and cover tightly. Cook over gently boiling water for 1 hour (knife inserted in the center will come out clean). Do not peek during cooking. Serve immediately. Yield: 4 servings.

CHICKEN MADRID

2	tablespoons margarine	30 mL
2	tablespoons cooking oil	30 mL
3	pound frying chicken, cut in pieces	1.5 kg
1	19-ounce can tomatoes	540 mL
1	cup chicken broth	250 mL
1	cup onion, sliced	250 mL
¼	cup parsley, chopped	50 mL
2	teaspoons salt	10 mL
¼	teaspoon pepper	1 mL
1	bay leaf	1
1	clove garlic, minced	1
1¼	cups uncooked rice	300 mL
1	12-ounce package frozen peas	340 g

Heat margarine and oil in large heavy saucepan. Add chicken pieces and brown well. Add tomatoes, chicken bouillon cube, water, onion, parsley, salt, pepper, bay leaf and garlic. Cover and cook over low heat for 30 minutes. Add rice, cook 30 minutes longer. Stir often. Add peas and cook until all moisture is absorbed.

CALICO BEAN CASSEROLE

A delicious variation of chili.

8	slices bacon	8
1	pound ground beef	.5 kg
1	medium onion, chopped	1
1	14-ounce can kidney beans	398 mL
1	14-ounce can beans with pork	398 mL
½	cup catsup	125 mL
2	tablespoons vinegar	30 mL
1	teaspoon Worcestershire sauce	5 mL
2	tablespoons brown sugar	30 mL
1	teaspoon prepared mustard	5 mL

Fry bacon until crisp; pour off grease and crumble bacon. Brown ground beef and onion. Combine bacon, ground beef and onion with remaining ingredients in 2½-quart (2.5 L) casserole. Bake at 325°F (160°C) for 2 hours. Yield: 6 servings.

POT LUCK SPECIAL

This favorite basic casserole goes with any meat dish at your buffet supper.

¼	cup chopped onion	50 mL
2	tablespoons margarine	25 mL
1	10-ounce can tomato soup	284 mL
½	cup water	125 mL
1	cup shredded cheddar cheese	250 mL
2	cups cooked macaroni	500 mL
2	tablespoons buttered bread crumbs	30 mL

Brown onion in margarine. Stir in soup, water and ¾ cup (200 mL) cheese. Heat till cheese melts. Blend with macaroni. Put into casserole. Sprinkle with remaining cheese and bread crumbs. Bake at 350°F (180°C) about 30 minutes or until nicely browned. Yield: 4 servings.

For a complete supper dish: Add 1 pound (.5 kg) fried sausage. Arrange macaroni and sausage in alternate layers. Bake 45 minutes. Yield: 4 servings.

QUICK SHEPHERD'S PIE

1	10-ounce can cream of mushroom soup	284 mL
1	pound ground beef	.5 kg
¼	cup onion, minced	50 mL
1	egg, beaten	1
¼	cup dry bread crumbs	50 mL
¼	teaspoon salt	1 mL
¼	teaspoon pepper	1 mL
2	cups mashed potatoes	500 mL
¼	cup cheddar cheese; grated	50 mL

Mix half of the soup with ground beef, onion, egg, crumbs, salt and pepper. Press into 9-inch (22.5 cm) pie plate. Bake at 350°F (180°C) for 25 minutes.

Remove from oven, drain off excess fat. Cover with mashed potatoes. Pour over remaining soup and bake 10 minutes. Sprinkle with grated cheese and pop back in oven for a few minutes. Yield: 6 servings

QUICK WIENER - POTATO SCALLOP

½	cup onion, chopped	125 mL
1	cup celery, chopped	250 mL
2	tablespoons fat	30 mL
2	tablespoons flour	30 mL
1	teaspoon salt	5 mL
¼	teaspoon pepper	1 mL
⅔	cup skim-milk powder	175 mL
3	cups water	750 mL
4	cups potatoes, sliced	1 L
1	cup carrots, shredded	250 mL
1	pound wieners, inch-sized (2.5 cm) pieces	.5 kg

Fry onion and celery in fat. Blend in flour, salt, pepper, milk powder. Gradually stir in water until thick and smooth. Add potatoes and carrots, simmer until tender. Add wieners and heat. Yield: 6 servings

SPAGHETTI PIE

This dish can be frozen for later use.

Crust:

6	ounces spaghetti	170 g
2	tablespoons butter	30 mL
⅓	cup Parmesan cheese	75 mL
2	eggs, well beaten	2

Filling:

1	pound ground beef	.5 kg
½	cup onion, chopped	125 mL
¼	cup green pepper, chopped	50 mL
1	cup canned tomatoes	250 mL
1	5½-ounce can tomato paste	156 mL
1	teaspoon sugar	5 mL
1	teaspoon oregano	5 mL
¼	teaspoon salt	1 mL
¼	teaspoon garlic powder	1 mL
1	cup cottage cheese	250 mL
½	cup Mozzarella cheese	125 mL

Cook spaghetti, drain and add butter, Parmesan cheese and eggs. Form into crust in 12-inch (30 cm) pizza plate. Brown meat, sauté onion and pepper, drain off fat. To these add tomatoes, tomato paste, sugar, oregano, salt, garlic powder. Spread cottage cheese over spaghetti crust. Cover with meat mixture; chill overnight.

Bake covered at 350°F (180°C) for 1 hour. Uncover, sprinkle with Mozzarella cheese and bake another 5 minutes. Cut into wedges and serve with green salad. Yield: 8 servings

SPEEDY BAKED BEANS

4	slices bacon	4
1	small onion, diced	1
1	green pepper, chopped	1
1	19-ounce can pineapple tid-bits	540 mL
2	14-ounce cans beans with pork	398 mL
2	tablespoons Worcestershire sauce	30 mL
½	cup brown sugar	125 mL
¾	cup catsup	200 mL

Fry bacon until crisp, then cook onion and green pepper until lightly browned. Drain off excess grease. Stir in remaining ingredients. Pour into greased casserole. Bake uncovered at 350°F (180°C) for 45 minutes. Yield: 8 servings

SALMON SPECIAL

1	15½-ounce can salmon	439 g
1	cup tomatoes	250 mL
2	eggs, well beaten	2
2	tablespoons lemon juice	30 mL
2	tablespoons butter, melted	30 mL
¼	teaspoon salt	1 mL
¼	teaspoon pepper	1 mL
2	cups cooked rice	500 mL

Empty salmon into a large bowl; break up larger pieces. Add remaining ingredients. Spoon into greased 1½-quart (1.5 L) casserole. Cover, bake at 375°F (190°C) for 1 hour. Yield 6 servings

SHIPWRECK

4	cups potatoes, thinly sliced	1000 mL
2	cups onions, sliced	500 mL
1½	pounds hamburger	.75 kg
2¼	cups rice	300 mL
1½	cups celery	375 mL
1½	cups carrots	375 mL
	Salt and pepper	
2	cans (28 ounces) tomatoes or	796 mL each can
2	cans (10 ounces) tomato soup	284 mL each can

plus 4 cans of hot water

Brown hamburger and remove fat. Into two casseroles of 2-quart (2 L) size place alternate layers of potatoes, onion, hamburger, uncooked rice, celery and carrots. Season with salt and pepper. Pour tomatoes or tomato soup mixed with water over ingredients. Bake for 2½ hours in the oven at 350°F. (180°C.) Each casserole serves 6 to 8.

TURKEY STROGANOFF

Use left-over turkey for a quick supper.

¼	cup green pepper, chopped	50 mL
2	tablespoons onions, chopped	30 mL
2	tablespoons margarine	30 mL
1	10-ounce can cream of mushroom soup	284 mL
½	cup sour cream	125 mL
¼	cup milk	50 mL
2	cups noodles, cooked	500 mL
1½	cups turkey, diced	375 mL
½	teaspoon paprika	2 mL

Fry pepper and onion in margarine. In 1-quart (1 L) casserole, blend soup, sour cream and milk; stir in remaining ingredients. Bake at 350°F (180°C) for 35 minutes. Yield: 4 servings

MEAT SAUCE

This sauce can be used immediately, refrigerated for several days, or frozen and used within two months.

2	pounds ground beef	1 kg
2	cloves garlic, minced	2
4	tablespoons catsup	60 mL
2	medium onions, minced	2
1	28-ounce can tomatoes	796 mL
2	7½ ounce cans tomato sauce	426 mL
1	10-ounce can mushroom pieces	284 mL
1	bay leaf	1
1	teaspoon oregano	5 mL
1	teaspoon salt	5 mL
½	teaspoon pepper	2 mL
1	beef bouillon cube	1 mL

Brown ground beef, garlic, catsup and onion. Add tomatoes. Stir in tomato sauce, mushroom pieces and liquid, seasoning and bouillon cube. Simmer 1 to 2 hours until thick.

Serve with spaghetti, noodles, in sloppy joes or lasagna. Yield: 8 cups (2 L)

CORN CASSEROLE

Serve this flavorful casserole with hot or cold roasted meat.

2	cups corn	500 mL
3	eggs, beaten	3
¼	cup celery, chopped	50 mL
¼	cup onion, chopped	50 mL
1½	cups tomatoes, diced	375 mL
1½	cups bread cubes, toasted	375 mL
2	teaspoons pepper	10 mL
1	tablespoon butter	15 mL

Mix corn and eggs, fold in remaining ingredients. Place in 1-quart (1 L) greased casserole. Cover and bake at 325°F (160°C) for 30 minutes. Garnish with paprika. Yield: 6 to 8 servings

TURNIP PUFF

Delicious served with turkey

3	cups cooked turnips, mashed	750 mL
2	tablespoons butter	30 mL
2	eggs	2
3	tablespoons flour	45 mL
1	tablespoon brown sugar	15 mL
1	teaspoon baking powder	5 mL
½	teaspoon salt	2 mL
¼	teaspoon pepper	1 mL
½	cup bread crumbs, buttered	125 mL

Combine turnip with butter. Beat eggs, add flour, sugar, baking powder, salt and pepper. Combine turnips with egg mixture, turn into 1½-quart (1.5 L) greased casserole. Top with buttered bread crumbs. Bake at 375°F (190°C) about 30 minutes. Yield: 6 to 8 servings

ETHNIC

I N PRESENTING this selection of ethnic recipes, Saskatchewan Women's Institute pays tribute to those individuals who came to the prairies from other lands, bringing with them their treasured recipes and handing them down from generation to generation. The traditional fare from those kitchens now enriches the cuisine for all.

Those who took up residence on the prairies came from many ethnic origins. Some sought to escape persecution; all longed to build up a home and economic security. But a melding of the diverse elements into a common denominator of culture and regional identity did not immediately take place. The prairies remained a mosaic and not a melting pot. Largely this was the result of group settlement of religious and ethnic communities. These groups maintained their distinctive culture and folkways, thereby preserving their culinary skills.

Saskatchewan history records the Ukrainian influence in north and west, the Barr colony of British settlers at Lloydminster, the German colony at Muenster, French at Gravelbourg, Mennonite settlements near Swift Current and Hungarians at Esterhazy. In Manitoba, the influence of Icelandic settlers is apparent in the community of Gimli, while Winkler is predominantly Mennonite. A strong Ukrainian presence is evident in northern Alberta and Cardston, to the south, is noted for its Mormon population. These people brought their own traditional ways of cooking, dishes originally associated with memories of familiar religious and family ceremonies and celebrations. Now, years after, the recipes are still passed along, perhaps to sustain cultural identity, certainly for pure enjoyment.

To celebrate the origins of these Canadians we give you the Frugt Suppe, a Swedish fruit cup, equally good as dessert or accompaniment to meat, a tasty Welsh leek soup, the Scottish Black bun, Ukrainian cabbage rolls and many, many more. Saskatchewan is the richer for this heritage and the good food of all groups is widely known and appreciated. The success of the Ukrainian perogy, a staple in the homeland, now a frozen convenience food available in every supermarket, is witness of such an acceptance.

14

HOT POTATO SALAD (German)

5	medium potatoes	5
4	slices bacon, diced	4
1	onion, chopped	1
1	tablespoon flour	15 mL
½	cup vinegar	125 mL
¼	cup water	65 mL
¼	cup sugar	65 mL
⅓	teaspoon dry mustard	1.5 mL
¼	teaspoon pepper	1 mL
1	teaspoon salt	5 mL
½	teaspoon celery seed	2 mL

Cook potatoes until tender, dice. Fry bacon until crisp; add to potatoes. Gently fry onion in bacon fat, stir in flour. Mix vinegar, water, sugar and seasonings together. Add to flour and onion mixture and bring to a boil. Pour over potatoes and bacon. Toss lightly to combine. Top with chopped parsley and paprika. Serve hot. Yield: 6 servings

HOT RICE SALAD (German)

Follow recipe for Hot Potato Salad with the following changes: Substitute two cups (500 mL) cooked rice for potatoes, add 2 tablespoons (30 mL) each of chopped green pepper and pimento. Omit mustard.

BORSCH (Ukrainian Chilled Beet Soup)

Serve in chilled bowls, garnish with thick sour cream; goes very well with meat loaf sandwiches.

3	medium beets, pared and sliced	3
2	tablespoons onion, minced	30 mL
2¾	cups water	675 mL
2	teaspoons cornstarch	10 mL
1	egg yolk, slightly beaten	1
2½	cups cream	625 mL
1	tablespoon lemon juice	15 mL
1	teaspoon Worcestershire sauce	5 mL
½	teaspoon salt	2 mL
¾	teaspoon celery salt	3 mL

Grind beets, using fine blade of food chopper. Place in large, heavy sauce pan. Add onion and 2½ cups (625 mL) water. Mix well. Bring to boil, then simmer for 30 minutes.

Remove from heat and while stirring constantly, add 2 cups (500 mL) of cream. Combine cornstarch with remaining ¼ cup (50 ml) of water. Stir into beet mixture. Return to heat and stir and cook 2 minutes. Combine egg yolk with remaining cream and blend into soup. Add seasonings, cool and store in refrigerator. Yield: 6 servings

YOGURT SOUP (Iranian)

This makes a delicious soup or it can be served as an appetizing drink.

1	hard boiled egg - chopped	1
3	cups plain yogurt	750 mL
½	cup light cream	125 mL
6	ice cubes	6
1	cucumber chopped	1
¼	cup green onion chopped	50 mL
2	teaspoons salt	10 mL
½	teaspoon pepper	2 mL
1	cup cold water	250 mL
	Garnish:	
1	tablespoon chopped parsley	15 mL
1	tablespoon fresh dill, chopped	15 mL

Mix first nine ingredients. Let stand in refrigerator 2-3 hours. Just before serving garnish with parsley and dill. The more finely chopped the ingredients, the better the soup.

TEA BISCUITS (English)

2	cups flour	500 mL
4	teaspoons baking powder	20 mL
¼	teaspoon cream of tartar	1 mL
½	teaspoon salt	2 mL
½	cup shortening	125 mL
¾	cup milk	175 mL

Sift flour, baking powder, cream of tartar and salt into a mixing bowl. With pastry blender or two knives, cut in shortening. Add milk gradually and using a fork blend lightly. Turn out on lightly floured surface and knead 8 to 10 times. Roll out to ½ inch (1.2 cm) thickness. Cut with floured 1¾ inch (4.5 cm) biscuit-cutter. Place on ungreased baking sheet. Bake at 450°F (230°C) for 10 to 12 minutes. Yield: 18 to 20 biscuits

TEA SCONES (Scottish)

Follow recipe for tea biscuits with the following additional in-gredients.

¾	cup raisins	175 mL
2	eggs, well beaten	2

Reduce milk to ½ cup (125 mL). Follow method for biscuits, adding raisins to dry ingredients and mixing eggs with milk. Divide dough into 2 portions. Pat into rounds ½ inch (1.2 cm) thick. Cut into 8 wedges or diamonds. Yield: 16 scones

BABKA (Ukrainian Easter Bread)

2	teaspoons sugar	10 mL
½	cup warm water	125 mL
2	packages yeast	16 g
4	eggs	4
6	egg yolks	6
1	cup sugar	250 mL
1	teaspoon salt	5 mL
⅓	cup fresh orange juice	75 mL
2	tablespoons orange rind, grated	30 mL
2	cups milk, scalded	500 mL
¾	cups butter, melted	175 mL
8-10	cups flour	2-2.5 L
2	cups raisins	500 mL
	fine bread crumbs	

Dissolve sugar in water; sprinkle in yeast. Let stand 10 minutes. Beat the eggs and egg yolks for 10 minutes, adding the sugar a little at a time. Add salt, orange juice, orange rind, milk and the yeast mixture. Mix well and add butter gradually. Add flour and continue mixing. Knead for 20 minutes or until dough no longer sticks to hands. Let rise in warm place until double in bulk.

Knead down and add raisins, let rise again.

Grease tall tins well and coat with bread crumbs. Form dough into ball small enough to fill ⅓ of the container. Let rise in a warm place until the dough barely reaches the top. Bake at 350°F (180°C) for 30 minutes. Yield: 4 loaves

OATMEAL SCONES (Isle of Lewis)

2	cups flour	500 mL
½	teaspoon salt	2 mL
2	cups oatmeal	500 mL
1	teaspoon baking soda	5 mL
1	cup buttermilk or sour milk	250 mL
6	tablespoons lard or	
	shortening	90 mL

Mix flour, salt and oatmeal thoroughly with pastry blender or two knives, cut in lard. Dissolve baking soda in milk. Add milk mixture and using a fork, blend lightly. Turn out on lightly floured surface and knead 8 to 10 times. Roll to ¼ inch (.6 cm) thickness. Cut into 4 inch (10 cm) squares. Place on ungreased baking sheet. Bake at 450°F (230°C) for 5 to 6 minutes. Return to oven for 5 to 6 minutes to brown other side. Set on edge to cool. Serve with butter and maple syrup or in place of bread with a meat dish. Store in tight container. Yield: 12 scones.

POTECA

Loaf can be used immediately but freezing improves its flavor.

Dough:

1	cup sour cream	250	mL
¼	cup milk	65	mL
¾	cup sugar	175	mL
1	teaspoon salt	5	mL
1	teaspoon sugar	5	mL
½	cup warm water	125	mL
2	packages yeast	16	g
6	cups flour	1.5	L
4	egg yolks, beaten	4	
½	cup margarine	125	mL

Filling:

1	pound almonds, finely chopped	.45	kg
4	egg whites	4	
¾	cup sugar	175	mL
1	teaspoon lemon rind	5	mL
¼	teaspoon salt	5	mL
	honey		

Combine sour cream, milk, sugar, and salt in a saucepan. Stir and heat slowly until sugar dissolves. Pour into large bowl to cool. Dissolve sugar in water, sprinkle in yeast and let stand 10 minutes.

Stir yeast into milk mixture; beat in half of the flour. Cover and let rise 45 minutes.

Beat to mix down. Beat egg yolks; add with margarine to dough. Knead in remainder of flour until smooth and elastic. Place in greased bowl, turn over to grease top of dough. Cover, let rise until double in bulk.

Punch down. Knead a few minutes and let rest 5 minutes. For the filling, beat egg whites foamy, add sugar, 1 tablespoon (15 ml) at a time until peaks form. Fold in nuts, rind and salt. Divide dough in half; on a lightly floured board roll each out into 26 x 10 inch (65 x 25 cm) rectangle. Spread nut filling over dough and roll up (jelly roll fashion) starting at long end. Place, seam down, in well-greased 9-inch (23 cm) angel-cake pan. Press ends to seal.

Cover pans, let rise 45 minutes or until almost double in bulk. Bake at 350°F (180°C) for 40 minutes until golden brown. Cool in pans on wire racks for 15 minutes. Loosen edges. Invert on racks to cool. Brush with honey. Garnish with nuts and cherries. Yield: 2 loaves

PULLA (Finnish Coffee Bread)

1	teaspoon water	5 mL
½	cup warm water	125 mL
1	package yeast	8 g
2	cups milk, scalded	500 mL
¾	cup sugar	175 mL
1	teaspoon salt	5 mL
⅓	cup butter	75 mL
2	teaspoons cardamon, ground	10 mL
6-7	cups flour	1.5-1.75 L
1	egg	1
1	tablespoon water	15 mL
¼	cup blanched almonds, chopped	50 mL

Dissolve sugar in water; sprinkle in yeast. Let stand 10 minutes. Pour milk into bowl, add sugar, salt, butter and cardamon. Stir until butter melts; add yeast. Beat in 2 cups (500 ml) flour. Knead in remainder of flour, turning out on a highly-floured surface to finish. Shape into a ball and place in greased bowl. Cover dough and let rise until doubled in size (about 2 hours).

Punch down, divide dough into four portions. Divide each portion into four pieces; shape each piece into a roll 15 inches (37.5 cm) long. Braid together. Place braided loaf on greased baking sheet. Repeat same procedure for the other 3 loaves. Cover and let rise again.

Beat egg and water, brush on loaves, sprinkle with almonds. Bake at 350°F (180°C) for 15 to 20 minutes. Yield: 4 loaves

HAIFA GLES (Jewish)

This is a meal you can prepare while making bread or buns.

12	buns, uncooked	12
8-10	lamb chops	8-10
¼	cup butter	65 mL
½	cup onion	125 mL
1	28-ounce can sauerkraut, drained	796 mL

Brown lamb chops. Sauté onions and sauerkraut in melted butter. Place this mixture in 9 x 13 inch (22.5 x 33 cm) baking dish. Arrange lamb chops on top and cover with risen buns. Bake at 350°F (180°C) for 30 minutes. Yield: 8 servings

NOODLES WITH SAUERKRAUT (Austrian)

2	cups flour	500 mL
3	teaspoons baking powder	45 mL
1	teaspoon salt	5 mL
1	cup water	250 mL
2	tablespoon fat	30 mL
3	cups water	750 mL
1	15-ounce can sauerkraut	426 mL

Mix together flour, baking powder, salt and water. Turn dough onto lightly floured surface; knead. Heat fat and water in an electric fry pan at 350°F (180°C). Using about 1 teaspoon (5 mL) of dough, form into thin oval-shaped noodles. If dough is too sticky, add more flour. Drop into liquid in frying pan (the noodles should be well covered with liquid). Place lid on pan and do not look for 15 minutes, or until you hear noodles frying. Now remove lid and loosen noodles. They should be crispy brown on bottom of pan. Stir and brown a little more. Add and mix heated sauerkraut, which has been frying in a separate pan. Serve while hot. Yield: 5 servings.

TOURTIÈRE (French Canadian Meat Pie)

Originally, this dish was prepared using pigeon (called "tourte" in France). Now, fresh pork or a mixture of meat is used. It is a French tradition to serve this dish on Christmas eve.

1	large potato	1
1	pound ground lean beef	.5 kg
1	pound ground lean pork	.5 kg
1	medium onion, chopped	1
1½	teaspoons salt	7 mL

½	teaspoon thyme	2 mL
½	teaspoon sage	2 mL
½	teaspoon dry mustard	2 mL
¼	teaspoon cloves	1 mL
	pastry for 2 9-inch (22.5 cm) pies	

Boil and mash potato, saving ½ cup (125 mL) of potato water. Set aside potato.

Mix all other ingredients with potato water in heavy saucepan. Bring to a boil and simmer, covered, about 40 minutes, or until tender. Remove from heat and add mashed potato. Mix well and chill.

Pour the meat mixture into pastry-lined pie plates. Cover with pastry, seal edges, and slash top crusts. Bake at 425°F (220°C) for 25 minutes. Yield: 12 to 14 servings

GASPÉ TOURTIÈRE (Acadian Meat Pie)

A tourtière with chicken as the main ingredient.

Filling:

1	chicken (3-4 pounds), cut up	1.5-2 kg
1	pound lean pork, cut in pieces	.5 kg
1	large onion, chopped	1
½	teaspoon allspice	2 mL
½	teaspoon savory	2 mL
	salt	
	pepper	
	dash of cinnamon	

Place all ingredients in large saucepan. Add sufficient water to cover chicken. Cover pan, and cook over low heat until chicken is tender. Cool, lift out chicken pieces, remove bones and skin. Chop, and mix well with pork mixture.

Pastry:

1¾	cups flour	425 mL
½	teaspoon salt	2 mL
4	teaspoons baking powder	20 mL
½	cup shortening	125 mL
⅔	cup milk	150 mL

Mix flour, salt, baking powder. Cut in shortening until crumbly. Stir in milk to make a soft dough. Roll or pat out on floured surface. Line two 9-inch (23 cm) pie plates with pastry. Fill with meat mixture. Cover with top crust, seal edges and slash. Bake at 350°F (180°C) for 45 minutes. Yield: 12 to 14 servings.

QUICHE LORRAINE (French)

A cheese and bacon custard pie, from the province of Lorraine, France.

1	9-inch (22.5 cm) pie shell, unbaked	1
6	slices bacon, crisply cooked	6
3	ounces Swiss cheese, grated	85 mL
4	eggs	4
1½	cups milk	375 mL
½	teaspoon salt	2 mL

Crumble bacon into pie shell, cover with cheese. Beat eggs, milk and salt together. Pour over bacon and cheese. Bake at 350°F (190°C) for 30 minutes until filling is brown and set. Serve immediately. Yield: 6 servings

SWEET AND SOUR SPARERIBS (Chinese)

After completion of the Canadian Pacific Railway in 1885, many Chinese left British Columbia and opened restaurants throughout the country. As a result, numerous recipes have been adapted to Canadian tastes.

2	pounds spareribs cut in 2½-inch pieces (5 cm)	1 kg
1	teaspoon brown sugar	5 mL
1	tablespoon soya sauce	15 mL
1	tablespoon catsup	15 mL
1	inch piece ginger root, cut-up	2.5 cm
1½	teaspoons cornstarch	7 mL
3	tablespoons water	45 mL
2	tablespoons cooking oil	30 mL

Place spareribs in large bowl and scald. Drain.

Place remaining ingredients (except oil) in a saucepan, mix well and simmer. Pour oil into shallow baking pan; add the spareribs, then pour over sauce. Bake at 375°F (190°C) for 15 minutes. Turn ribs and continue cooking at 275°F (135°C) for 40 minutes or until meat is tender and begins to pull away from bones. Turn often. Yield: 4 servings

CHOP SUEY (Chinese - Canadian)

North American in origin but with a satisfying Oriental taste.

1-2	pounds ground beef	.5-1 kg
1	10-ounce can consomme	284 mL
1	cup onion, chopped	250 mL
4	cups celery, chopped	1 L
1	cup cabbage (optional), chopped	250 mL
1	10-ounce can mushrooms	284 mL
1	14-ounce can bean sprouts	398 mL
	Or	
1	19-ounce can Chinese vegetables	540 mL
3	tablespoons soya sauce	45 mL
1	tablespoon cornstarch	15 mL

Brown beef in large heavy skillet. Pour over consomme, simmer 5 minutes. Add onion, celery, cabbage, mushrooms, bean sprouts (or chinese vegetables) and 1 tablespoon (15 mL) soya sauce. Just before serving add cornstarch mixed with remaining soya sauce. Simmer until sauce is thick.

Serve over rice, topped with noodles. Yield: 6 servings

BEAN PLAKI (Greek Baked Beans)

1	pound beans	.5 kg
1	cup olive or cooking oil	250 mL
2	tablespoons tomato paste	30 mL
3	medium onions, sliced	3
2	carrots, diced	2
2	stalks celery, diced	2
½	teaspoon salt	2 mL
½	teaspoon pepper	2 mL
	minced parsley to taste	

Wash beans, soak overnight.

Drain beans, bring to a boil and skim. Add all other ingredients. Cook and simmer gently for about 2 hours until beans are tender. Yield: 8 servings

PIZZA (Italian-Canadian)

Crust:

1	teaspoon sugar	5 mL
1 ¼	cups warm water	315 mL
1	package yeast	8 g
2	tablespoons oil	30 mL
1	teaspoon salt	5 mL
4	cups flour	1 L

Topping:

Mozzarella cheese slices, mushrooms, bacon bits, summer sausage slices, green pepper chunks.

Sauce:

2	7½-ounce cans tomato sauce	426 mL
1	5½-ounce can tomato paste	156 mL
¼	cup water	60 mL
⅓	cup cooking oil	75 mL
¼	teaspoon pepper	1 mL
1	teaspoon oregano	5 mL
1	teaspoon salt	5 mL
1	clove, garlic, minced	1
4	tablespoons Parmesan cheese, grated	60 mL

Dissolve sugar in water, sprinkle in yeast. Stir in oil and salt, then mix in flour. Knead on floured board until smooth. Place in greased bowl, let rise 1½ hours.

Knead lightly, divide dough into two parts, and place on greased baking sheets. With palm of hand press out dough into circles 12 inches (30 cm) in diameter, let rise.

Place topping over dough. Mix tomato sauce, tomato paste, water, oil with pepper, oregano, salt and garlic to make sauce. Place half of sauce on each pizza. Sprinkle with Parmesan cheese. Bake at 400°F (200°C) for 20 to 25 minutes. Yield: 2 12-inch (30 cm) pizzas.

LAZY HOLUBTSI (Ukrainian)

8	slices bacon	8
1	cup leftover ham, sausage or meatballs	250 mL
1	medium onion, chopped	1
3	cups cooked rice	750 mL
1	15-ounce can sauerkraut	426 mL
½	cup water	125 mL
½	teaspoon salt	2 mL
½	teaspoon pepper	2 mL

Fry bacon until crisp, add onion and brown. Pour off fat. Stir in remaining ingredients (including liquid from sauerkraut), cover and simmer for 10 minutes. Yield: 6 servings.

PEROGIES (Ukrainian)

These may be frozen and cooked later.

Dough:

3	cups flour	750 mL	
½	teaspoon salt	2 mL	
¾	cup warm water	175 mL	
2	tablespoons cooking oil	30 mL	
1	egg	1	
1	tablespoon vinegar	15 mL	

Filling:

6	medium potatoes, cooked, mashed	6	
1	bag dry cottage cheese	500	g
1	carton creamed cottage cheese	500	g
1	tablespoon onion, chopped	15 mL	
	salt to taste		

Sift flour and salt into bowl, add water, oil, egg and vinegar. Mix well until smooth and elastic. Roll dough thin; cut into 3-inch (7.5 cm) squares. Mix potato, cheeses, onion and salt for filling. Fill each square with 1 tablespoon (15 mL) of filling; fold and pinch together. Place on a dry tea towel as you prepare them and put a damp tea towel over the top.

Drop perogies into boiling salted water; stir with a wooden spoon to prevent sticking. Boil 4 to 5 minutes. Place in colander to drain, then put in bowl and pour melted butter over top. Serve with sour cream or mushroom sauce.

ASPARAGUS (Norwegian)

1	pound asparagus spears	.5 kg
⅓	cup butter or margarine	75 mL
2	tablespoons bread crumbs	30 mL
1	tablespoon parsley, minced	15 mL
1	hard-cooked egg, chopped	1

Cook asparagus by tying spears in bunches and standing up in a narrow pot with water halfway up the stalks. This cooks the tough portion more completely. Brown butter in skillet, add bread crumbs and parsley. Arrange asparagus on platter, top with sauce and garnish with egg. Yield: 6 servings

KARTOFFELPUFFER (Austrian Potato Patties)

3	cups peeled and grated potatoes	750 mL
1	tablespoon flour	15 mL
1	egg, beaten	1
½	teaspoon salt	2 mL
¼	teaspoon pepper	1 mL
2	tablespoons fat	30 mL

Place grated potato in a bowl, add flour, egg, salt and pepper. In a large frying pan heat the fat. Spread ¾ cups (175 mL) of batter evenly over bottom of pan. Fry until golden brown and crisp on both sides. Yield: 4 servings

SCOTCH EGGS

5	eggs, hard-boiled	5
1	pound sausage meat	.5 kg
1	egg, beaten	1
	bread crumbs	
	fat for deep-frying	

Shell eggs and dry. Divide sausage meat into five portions. On a floured board flatten each piece into a round big enough to cover the egg. Work meat around each egg until the egg is completely encased in a smooth layer of meat. Dip into beaten egg and roll in bread crumbs. Fry in deep fat for 3 to 4 minutes until golden brown. Cut in half, serve either hot or cold. Yield: 5 servings

RULLA PYLSA (Icelandic Rolled Spiced Lamb)

This is a good meat dish for a buffet supper. Icelanders also slice it thinly and serve it on buttered, brown bread for open-face sandwiches.

2	pounds lamb, flank	1 kg
1	medium onion, minced	1
2	teaspoons salt	10 mL
2	teaspoons brown sugar	10 mL
1	teaspoon ground cloves	5 mL
1	teaspoon allspice	5 mL
½	teaspoon saltpetre	2 mL
½	teaspoon pepper	2 mL

Mix onion with spices. Prepare lamb flank by wiping with damp cloth, removing membranes and trimming to rectangular shape and size. Place flank on board, skin side down. Spread with onion and spices. Roll tightly, sew the ends and along the edge closely. Wrap firmly in cheesecloth, refrigerate for 7 days, turning daily.

Remove cloth; place meat roll in kettle and cover with cold water. Bring to boil, skim. Cover and simmer 2½ hours or until tender. Place in loaf pan, under a heavy weight; chill overnight.

Alternate method:

After the rolled flank has been tied firmly, soak it in brine for 8 days.

Brine:

2	quarts water	2 L
1	cup salt	250 mL
½	cup brown sugar	125 mL
½	teaspoon saltpetre	2 mL

Remove from brine, rinse off and wipe clean. Place in fresh water and simmer until tender. Place in loaf pan under a heavy weight and chill.

PORK CHOPS NAPOLI (Italian)

6	pork chops	6
2	tablespoons cooking oil	30 mL
1	cup tomato sauce	250 mL
¼	cup green olives, chopped	50 mL
1	green pepper, sliced in wedges	1
1	10-ounce can mushrooms, drained	284 mL

Brown pork chops in oil. Add tomato sauce, olives and pepper. Bring to boil; reduce heat, and simmer covered for 1½ hours or until chops are tender. Add mushrooms and simmer 5 minutes. Yield: 6 servings.

BLACK BUN (Scottish)

This cake should be made several weeks before it is to be used so that it can mature and mellow. Black Bun always appears on Hogmanay (New Year's Eve).

Cake:

3	cups flour	750 mL
½	cup sugar	125 mL
1	tablespoon cloves	15 mL
2	tablespoons cinnamon	30 mL
2	tablespoons ginger	30 mL
1	teaspoon allspice	5 mL
½	teaspoon black pepper	2 mL
1	teaspoon baking soda	5 mL
2	pounds currants	1 kg
2	pounds raisins	1 kg
½	pound mixed peel	227 g
½	pound almonds, blanched	227 g
2	tablespoons brandy (optional)	30 mL
1	egg, beaten	1
1¼	cup milk	300 mL

Pastry:

3	cups flour	750 mL
1	cup butter	250 mL
	water to mix	
1	egg, beaten	1

Sift together the dry ingredients and add the prepared fruit and almonds. Mix brandy, egg and milk. Add to flour-fruit mixture and mix just to moisten.

To prepare pastry, cut the butter into the flour and add just enough water to make a stiff dough. Roll thin. Grease a large cake tin and line it evenly with pastry. Pour in the fruit mixture. Roll out another circle of pastry to cover the top. Moisten edges of pastry with water. Place pastry over top and seal edges. Prick top with a fork and brush with beaten egg. Bake at 350°F (180°C) for 3 to 4 hours.

POPPY SEED CHIFFON CAKE
(Ukrainian-Canadian)

½	cup poppy seeds	125 mL
1	cup boiling water	250 mL
7	egg whites	7
½	teaspoon cream of tartar	2 mL
2	cups flour	500 mL
3	teaspoons baking powder	15 mL
1½	cups sugar	375 mL
1	teaspoon salt	5 mL
½	cup cooking oil	125 mL
2	teaspoons vanilla	10 mL
7	egg yolks	7
¼	teaspoon baking soda	1 mL

Soak poppy seeds in water, let stand for 2 hours.

Place egg whites in large glass bowl, add cream of tartar; beat until mixture forms very stiff peaks. In a separate bowl mix flour, baking powder, sugar and salt. Stir in oil, vanilla, egg yolks, baking soda and poppy seed mixture. Beat until smooth. Gently pour egg yolk mixture over egg whites. Fold in (do not stir). Pour into ungreased large tube pan. Bake at 325°F (160°C) for 50 minutes then at 350°F (180°C) for 10 minutes more. Invert pan to cool. When cool, remove from pan. Dust icing sugar over cake (or frost with favorite icing).

SCHNITZ PIE (Pennsylvania Dutch)

In 1800 Mennonite families from Pennsylvania settled in the forest on the banks of Grand River, Waterloo County, Ontario. At that time dried apples were used in Schnitz pie but today fresh apples add a zesty appeal to this traditional dessert.

1	9-inch (22.5 cm) pie shell, unbaked	1
5	cups apples, peeled, quartered	1.25 L
1	cup sour cream	250 mL
2	tablespoons flour	20 mL
¾	cup sugar	175 mL
3	tablespoons butter	45 mL
1	teaspoon cinnamon	5 mL

Prepare pie shell. Arrange apples attractively in pie shell. Pour sour cream over apples. Mix flour, sugar, butter, cinnamon; sprinkle over pie. Bake at 325°F (160°C) about 45 minutes until apples are cooked and custard is firm. Yield: 6 servings.

KOURABIEDES (Greek Shortbread)

1½	cups butter	375 mL
1	cup fruit sugar	250 mL
2	egg yolks	2
1	teaspoon baking powder	5 mL
1	teaspoon vanilla	5 mL
3½	cups flour	875 mL

Cream butter with electric mixer. Add sugar and egg yolks; beat seven minutes. Add baking powder, vanilla and flour. Mix well. Shape into fingers 3 x ¾ inch (7.5 x 2 cm). Bake at 325°F (160°C) about 15 minutes or until lightly browned. Roll in icing sugar while still warm. Yield: 60 cookies.

APFELSINEN ODER ZITRONENESCHNITTEN
(German Orange or Lemon Slice)

Dough:

2	cups flour	500 mL
1	teaspoon baking powder	5 mL
⅓	cup sugar	75 mL
1	egg, beaten	1
1	teaspoon vanilla	5 mL
½	cup butter or margarine	125 mL

Lemon filling:

1⅓	cup almonds	325 mL
4	tablespoons lemon juice	60 mL
4	teaspoons lemon rind, grated	20 mL
⅔	cup sugar	150 mL

Orange filling:

1½	cups walnuts, chopped	375 mL
4	tablespoons orange juice	60 mL
4	teaspoons orange rind, grated	20 mL
⅔	cup sugar	150 mL

Glaze:

2	tablespoons icing sugar	30 mL
1	tablespoon water	15 mL

Prepare filling by mixing together fruit, juice, nuts and sugar. Use either lemon **or** orange filling recipe.

Sift flour, baking powder and sugar into a bowl. Add egg and vanilla. Stir. Cut in butter and mix well. Turn out on a lightly-floured surface and knead. Divide into 2 parts. Flatten one part, fit into an 8-inch (20 cm) square pan. Place filling on dough. Cover with the second part of dough. Pierce with a fork. Bake at 350°F (180°C) for 25 minutes. Pour on a glaze of icing sugar and water.

SHORTBREAD (Scottish)

Traditional Scottish shortbreads frequently contained rice flour and castor sugar.

2	cups butter	500 mL
1	cup icing sugar	250 mL
4	cups flour	1 L

Cream butter until very light. Sift sugar and add to butter. Gradually stir in flour. Knead well to blend in last of flour. Chill for 30 minutes.

Roll dough on lightly-floured surface to ¼ inch (.6 cm) thickness and cut into fancy shapes or roll into 2 circles ½ inch (1.2 cm) thick. Prick with fork. Bake on ungreased cookie sheet at 350°F (180°C) for about 20 minutes until firm. Allow 1½ hours baking time for circles. Yield: 50 cookies or two circles.

ZSERBO SYELET (Hungarian Walnut Slice)

This slice freezes well.

Dough:

1	teaspoon sugar	5 mL
⅔	cup warm water	150 mL
½	package yeast	4 g
2½	cups flour	625 mL
1	teaspoon baking powder	5 mL
1½	cups sugar	375 mL
1	cup margarine	250 mL
1	egg	1
2	tablespoons cream	30 mL

Filling:

2	cups walnuts, ground	500 mL
⅔	cup icing sugar	150 mL
2	teaspoons lemon rind, grated	10 mL
2	cups jam	500 mL

Dissolve sugar in water; sprinkle in yeast. Let stand for 10 minutes. Mix flour, baking powder, sugar and margarine to fine crumb stage. Add egg to yeast then pour all into flour and stir to form a soft dough. If dough is stiff, add cream.

Mix walnuts, sugar and lemon rind.

Divide dough in three parts. On a floured board roll dough to fit 9 x 13 inch (22 x 33 cm) pan. Cover with jam and half of the walnut filling. Roll out second part, put in pan on top of first layer, again cover with jam and walnut filling. Roll out remaining dough and cover pan completely, finishing the edge as for pie. Prick with a fork and let rise 1 hour. Bake at 350°F (180°C) for 30 minutes or until done. Remove from oven and frost.

FATTIGMAND (Norwegian Cookies)

Fattigmand, literally translated means poor man's cake. In Scandinavian countries in earlier times even the poor man had the ingredients for making fine food; he had cattle, pigs and chickens, and was therefore assured a supply of lard, eggs, butter, milk, cheese and meats.

6	egg yolks	6
4	tablespoons sugar	60 mL
1	tablespoon butter, melted	15 mL
¼	teaspoon salt	1 mL
6	tablespoons whipping cream	90 mL
¼	teaspoon ground cardamon	1 mL
3	cups flour	750 mL

Beat egg yolks thoroughly; add sugar and mix well. Add melted butter, salt and cream. Stir in cardamon and 2½ cups (625 mL) of flour. Use extra ½ cup (125 mL) flour to make a dough of rolling consistency. Roll very thin. Cut in 2½-inch (6.2 cm) strips on slant; cut in 2½-inch (6.2 cm) strips the other direction to make diamonds. Cut a slit in the center of each diamond, pull the end through the slit. Fry in deep fat at 370°F (190°C) for 2 to 3 minutes until golden brown. Dust with powdered sugar. Yield: 100 cookies.

BERLINER KRANSER (Norwegian Wreath Cookie)

Delicious and buttery, these gay little wreaths are made each holiday season in Norway.

1½	cups shortening (half-butter)	375 mL	
1	cup sugar	250 mL	
2	teaspoons orange rind	10 mL	
2	eggs	2	
4	cups flour	1	L
1	egg white	1	
2	tablespoons icing sugar	30 mL	
	cherries		

Cream butter, add sugar and orange rind; beat until light and fluffy. Add egg. Gradually add flour, beating constantly. It may be easier to fold in last of flour while mixing by hand. Cover dough and chill. Take small amount of dough, roll pencil - thin into 6–inch (15 cm) long strip. Form into circle, overlapping ends. Beat egg white, add icing sugar. Brush cookies with egg mixture. Decorate with a piece of cherry. Place on greased cookie sheet. Bake at 350°F (180°C) for 15 minutes until lightly browned. Yield: 72 cookies

VANILLA KRANSER (Norwegian Vanilla Wreaths)

Follow recipe for Berliner Kranser with the following changes: Substitute 2 teaspoons (10 mL) vanilla for orange rind. After last of flour is mixed in, add ¼ pound (125 g) finely-chopped almonds.

NURNBURGERS (Norwegian Cookies)

There is no shortening in this recipe so it is necessary to "mellow" cookies for several days by storing in an airtight container.

1	cup honey	250 mL
¾	cup brown sugar	175 mL
1	egg	1
1	teaspoon lemon rind	5 mL
1	tablespoon lemon juice	15 mL
2¾	cups flour	675 mL
½	teaspoon soda	2 mL
1	teaspoon cinnamon	5 mL
½	teaspoon allspice	2 mL
½	teaspoon nutmeg	2 mL
¼	teaspoon cloves	1 mL
⅓	cup cut peel	75 mL
⅓	cup almond halves	75 mL
⅓	cup cherries, sliced	75 mL

Heat honey to boiling point; cool. Stir in sugar, egg, lemon rind and lemon juice. Add all dry ingredients. Mix in peel. Chill dough overnight.

Roll out dough ¼ inch (.6 cm) thick. Cut in 2-inch (5 cm) rounds. Place on greased cookie sheet. To make "daisy-like" cookies, press almonds around edges of dough and place cherry in center. Bake at 350°F (180°C) for about 10 minutes, until set. Yield: 72 cookies

SANDBAKELSE (Norwegian Sand Tarts)

Fragile almond-flavored shells, made in Sandbakelse pans or in tiny fluted tart forms.

1	pound butter	500 mL
1	cup brown sugar	250 mL
1	cup white sugar	250 mL
1	egg	1
10	drops almond extract	10
6	cups flour	1.5 L

Cream butter, add sugars and cream together thoroughly. Add egg and vanilla. Gradually work in the flour. Take a small piece of dough and press firmly into sandbakelse pans, spreading dough as thinly as possible. Bake at 350°F (180°C) for 10 minutes until light brown. Cool and carefully remove from pans (tap moulds on table or slip a knife between tarts and tin to aid removal from pans). Yield: 70 cookies

HOMENTASHEN (Jewish)

Dough:

4	cups flour	1 L
3	tablespoons baking powder	45 mL
½	teaspoon salt	2 mL
3	eggs	3
1	cup sugar	250 mL
¾	cup cooking oil	175 mL
⅓	cup fresh orange juice	75 mL
1	egg white, beaten	1

Filling:

2	cups dates	500 mL
¼	cup water	65 mL
1	cup walnuts, chopped	250 mL
1	teaspoon vanilla	5 mL

Sift flour, baking powder, and salt together. Beat eggs until light and lemon-colored. Add sugar gradually, and beat until thick. Add oil. Add dry ingredients alternately with orange juice. Mix well.

Prepare filling by cooking dates in water. Cool, put through a sieve. Add walnuts, and vanilla and mix well.

Roll dough thinly on lightly floured surface. Cut into 2-inch (5 cm) rounds. Put a spoonful of filling on each round. Fold, pinching edges together. Brush with egg white. Place on greased baking dish. Bake at 350°F (180°C) for 15 minutes.

RICH ROHALYKY (Ukrainian Easter Fare)

This recipe gives tender, glossy and very tasty rohalyky. Although yeast is used in this recipe the dough should not rise as it would normally. Filling may be varied—prepared poppy seed, cottage cheese or jam.

Dough:

1	teaspoon sugar	5 mL
½	cup lukewarm water	125 mL
1	package yeast	8 g
2¾	cups flour	685 mL
2	tablespoons sugar	30 mL
½	teaspoon salt	2 mL
1	cup butter, chilled	250 mL
1	egg, beaten	1
	cherry halves	
	egg white, beaten	
	walnuts, chopped	

Cottage cheese filling

1	bag dry cottage cheese	500 g
2	eggs	2
2	teaspoons margarine	10 mL
	salt	

Mix together well.

Poppy seed filling

½	cup poppy seed	125 mL
2	tablespoons sugar	30 mL
	salt	
	pepper	

Scald poppy seed, drain. Cover with warm water, soak 30 minutes. Drain thoroughly through a fine strainer. Grind with fine blade of a food chopper. Add sugar, salt, pepper and mix well.

To make dough, dissolve sugar in water; sprinkle in yeast. Let stand 10 minutes. Sift flour, sugar and salt. Grate the hard, chilled butter in short strips on the coarse grater, combine with the flour mixture and keep cold. Add egg to the dissolved yeast, combine with the flour mixture, knead the dough lightly but not to smoothness. Cover with wax paper and chill for 1 hour.

Roll the dough to ¼ inch (.6 cm) thickness on a floured board. Cut into 2½-inch (6.2 cm) squares. Put 1 teaspoon (5 mL) of cottage cheese or poppy seed filling in center of squares. Fold 2 opposite corners to overlap ½ inch (1.2 cm) at center. Place half a cherry in the opposite two corners close to the filling. Place on greased pan and chill ½ hour.

Preheat oven to to 450°F (230°C). Brush the squares with beaten egg white and sprinkle with chopped nuts. Place in oven and immediately turn oven to 400°F (200°C). Bake 12 minutes. Yield: 35 cookies.

PERISHKI, Also PYRIZHKZ (Ukrainian, Polish)

This filled, pastry-type turnover was claimed both by Ukrainian and Polish settlers. The original recipe called for rolling dough into marble-sized pieces, chilling overnight and rolling out the next day. This modern version can be prepared in a shorter period of time.

	Dough:	
2	cups flour	500 mL
1	cup butter or margarine	250 mL
3	egg yolks	3
2	tablespoons sour cream	30 mL
2	teaspoons vanilla	30 mL
2	teaspoons lemon juice	10 mL
⅓	cup jam	75 mL
½	cup walnuts, chopped	125 mL
	Meringue:	
3	egg whites	3
1	teaspoon sugar	5 mL
	walnut halves	

Mix flour and shortening together. Beat egg yolks, cream vanilla, lemon juice until fluffy. Add to flour mixture. Chill dough thoroughly.

On a lightly-floured surface roll dough to pie crust thickness. Cut with 2½-inch (6.2 cm) cookie-cutter. Mix together jam and walnuts. Place a little jam-walnut mixture in center of circle. Moisten edges and fold into a turnover. Bake at 350°F (180°C) until lightly browned.

To make the meringue, beat egg whites until stiff; add sugar. Place a spoonful on the top of each turnover and decorate with a walnut. Bake until meringue is brown. Yield: 5 dozen

LEMON SCHAUM TORTE (Austria)

Meringue shell:

4	egg whites	4
½	teaspoon cream of tartar	2 mL
1	cup sugar	250 mL

Lemon custard filling

4	egg yolks	4
½	cup sugar	125 mL
3	tablespoons lemon juice	45 mL
2	teaspoons lemon rind, grated	10 mL
1	cup whipping cream	250 mL

Beat egg whites until frothy, add cream of tartar. Beat until egg whites form soft peaks. Beat in the sugar gradually, a little at a time, until the meringue is stiff and glossy. Pour into well-greased and floured 8-inch (20 cm) round layer pan. Bake at 275°F (135°C) for 20 minutes; increase temperature to 300°F (150°C) and continue baking for 40 minutes. Remove from pan immediately to prevent sticking. Cool.

To make filling, beat egg yolks until thick and lemon-colored. Beat in sugar gradually, add lemon juice and rind. Cook in double boiler about 5 minutes until custard is thick. Chill.

Whip cream. Spread half of the whipped cream over cooled meringue shell. Pour in custard filling and cover with remainder of the whipped cream. Chill 24 hours.

Serve in wedge-shaped pieces. Yield: 6 servings.

PERFECT SCOTTISH TRIFLE

This import from the British Isles is a popular dessert — perhaps because it makes left-over cake glamorous.

2½	cups milk	625 mL
¼	cup sugar	65 mL
3	egg yolks	3
1	tablespoon corn starch	15 mL
1	teaspoon vanilla	5 mL
	sponge cake or white cake	
½	cup sherry or juice	125 mL
1	15-ounce package frozen	425 g
	raspberries	
½	cup whipping cream	125 mL

Scald milk, add sugar. Beat eggs until light, add cornstarch. Gradually stir in milk mixture. Return to saucepan, cook over low heat, stirring constantly until custard coats a metal spoon. Remove from heat, stir in vanilla. Chill.

In a large bowl arrange cake cut in pieces ¾ inch (2 cm) thick. Sprinkle with ¼ cup (65 mL) sherry or fruit juice. Spoon custard over cake; top with thawed raspberries. Add remainder of sherry or fruit juice. Chill overnight.

Serve with whipped cream. Yield: 8 servings.

PEACH MELBA (English)

Dame Nellie Melba (1861-1931), an Australian soprano often sang at Covent Garden, England. After one of her performances she had supper at the Savoy Hotel where the chef created this dessert made of peaches and raspberries and called it Peach Melba in her honor.

½	cup peach syrup	125 mL
8	rounds of sponge cake	8
1	teaspoon lemon juice	5 mL
1	pint vanilla ice cream	½ L
	Whipped cream	
2-3	tablespoons raspberry jam	30 - 45 mL
1	teaspoon gelatin	5 mL
	few drops red food coloring	
8	peach halves	8
	chopped nuts	

Boil the peach syrup for a few minutes, then pour a little over each round of sponge cake. Put jam, gelatin and lemon juice into saucepan with remaining syrup. Heat gently over a pan of hot water to dissolve gelatin. Strain mixture and tint with red food coloring. Put a round of cake into each sundae dish, cover with a spoonful of ice cream, then half a peach. Pour sauce over. Top with whipped cream and nuts. Yield: 8 servings.

STEAMED APPLE NUDELS (German)

6	cups flour	1.5 L
3	teaspoons baking powder	15 mL
1	teaspoon salt	5 mL
3	eggs	3
2	cups milk	500 mL
	apples, chopped	
¼	cup sugar	60 mL
2	cups hot water	500 mL
½	cup butter	125 mL

Mix together flour, baking powder and salt; add eggs and milk to make a stiff dough. Divide dough into 4 parts. Place each part on lightly floured surface and roll out into a rectangle. Dough should be thin. Cover dough with apples and sprinkle with a little sugar. Put water and butter in electric fry pan at 350°F (180°C). In it place the pieces of dough. Cover and cook for 1 hour. When water has evaporated and noodles begin to fry, turn off heat. Leave for 5 minutes. Serve hot.

APFELKUCHEN (German Apple Cake)

1	cup butter	250 mL
1	cup sugar	250 mL
2	eggs, beaten	2
2	cups flour	500 mL
1	teaspoon baking powder	5 mL
1	cup milk	250 mL
7	apples, peeled, sliced	7
1	cup sugar	250 mL

Cream butter, add sugar and eggs; stir well. Add flour and baking powder. Mix well until stiff and crumbly; add milk slowly to make a heavy creamy dough. Spread dough on large baking sheet. Arrange apples on top of dough. Bake at 350°F (180°C) for 40 to 45 minutes. During the last 10 minutes of baking sprinkle sugar over cake. Yield: 8 servings.

SZILVAS GOMBOC (Hungarian Plum Dumplings)

A tasty dessert, best when made with ripe prune plums.

12-14	plums	12-14
2	eggs	2
¼	cup white sugar	65 mL
1	cup milk	250 mL
3	cups flour	750 mL
1	teaspoon baking powder	5 mL
¾	teaspoon salt	3 mL

Pit plums without separating the halves completely. Beat together eggs and sugar, add the milk. Slowly add the sifted dry ingredients. This should make a soft dough. Roll dough out on a floured board to a thickness of ¼ inch (.6 cm). Cut into 12 to 14 squares (bigger than the plums). Put a plum in the center of each square and seal the dough securely to make round, water-tight dumplings. Drop a few at a time into boiling water; cook 15 minutes. If dumplings stick to the bottom of the saucepan, prod gently until they rise. Remove from the water; serve with hot butter or cream and sugar. Yield: 6 servings.

FRUGT SUPPE (Swedish Fruit Soup)

This can be served cold with cream as a dessert, or with cold meat. Serve hot accompanying Chinese foods or a meat fondue.

½	cup tapioca	125 mL
1	cup water	250 mL
1	cup prunes	250 mL
½	cup dried apricots	125 mL
3	tablespoons lemon juice	30 mL
2	teaspoons lemon rind, grated	10 mL
1	stick cinnamon	1
1	cup sugar	250 mL
4	cups water	1 L

Soak tapioca overnight in one cup of water.

In the morning, add fruits, cinnamon, sugar and remainder of water. Cook until fruit is soft. Yield: 8 servings.

For Finnish Fruit Soup: Increase prunes to 2 cups (500 mL) and substitute 1 cup (250 mL) raisins for the dried apricots.

MINCEMEAT (English)

In the early days in Canada, mincemeat contained meat, but English mincemeat does not. Cooks in both countries do agree that mincemeat pie should be served in the Christmas season.

4	pounds apples	2 kg
3	pounds brown sugar	1.5 kg
2	cups beef suet	500 mL
	Or	
1⅔	cups margarine	400 mL
1	pound raisins	500 g
1	pound currants	500 g
1	cup mixed peel	250 mL
3	tablespoons nutmeg	45 mL
2	tablespoons cinnamon	30 mL
½	cup lemon juice	125 mL
2	tablespoons lemon rind, grated	30 mL

Grind suet through fine blade in food chopper. Core and quarter apples; grind with raisins, currants and peel through medium blade in food chopper. Mix thoroughly with remainder of ingredients. Keep in refrigerator or store in freezer. Yield: 4 pints.

VINARTERTA (Icelandic)

Named for an opera that was playing in Vienna, but it came to be called Vinarterta meaning Viennese torte.

Dough:

1	cup butter	250 mL
1½	cups sugar	375 mL
2	eggs	2
2	tablespoons cream	30 mL
1	teaspoon almond flavoring	5 mL
1	teaspoon baking powder	5 mL
4	cups flour	1 L
¼	teaspoon salt	1 mL

Filling:

1	pound prunes	.5 kg
1	cup water	250 mL
1	cup sugar	250 mL
½	teaspoon cinnamon	2 mL
½	teaspoon cardamon, finely ground	2 mL

Cream butter, work in sugar until well blended, add eggs one at a time. Add cream, almond flavoring and beat well. Combine baking powder, flour, and salt and work into butter mixture.

Divide dough into 5 parts. Roll one part at a time on bottom of 9-inch (22.5 cm) lightly greased layer cake tin. Bake at 350°F (180°C) until lightly brown. Cool the sheets of dough after baking.

Simmer prunes and water until liquid is absorbed. Cool, remove stones, put prunes through food chopper. Combine with one cup (250 mL) sugar, cinnamon, cardamon, cook over low heat for 15 minutes. Cool. Put filling between layers of cooked dough, (top layer to be dough).

This cake moistens as it ages. To cut cake, cut in 1 inch (2.5 cm) strips, then cut each strip into 2- or 3-inch (5 cm) sections. Cake can be cut and then frozen.

PIONEER

THE FIRST pioneers who came to the prairies came to a harsh land, a land where nature reluctantly yielded up bounty only to those who worked and survived the rigors of climate and isolation.

For some of those who came early with little money, the only food during the first winter was oatmeal, tea and rabbits. As soon as possible they acquired a cow so there might be milk. Bannock, biscuits and porridge made from ground wheat were common fare. For settlers who were getting established, staple groceries were flour, dried beans, prunes, corn syrup and perhaps canned milk, black strap molasses and dried apples. The diet was supplemented with eggs, salt pork and potatoes produced on the farm.

The pioneer woman who had never before made bread soon learned, not only to feed her own family, but to help out the lonely bachelors and weary travellers passing by on their way to find their own homesteads. At first, bread was made with a starter that was carefully tended and kept active for weeks. When dried yeast cakes appeared on the market, the starter was joyfully abandoned. Farm women made butter, cured the meat and made the family soap with rendered fat. They soon discovered the wild fruits of the prairie: Saskatoons, chokecherries, wild strawberries and raspberries. Wild game and fish sometimes helped to relieve the monotony. Vegetables were grown in large quantities: potatoes, turnips, beets and carrots. Rhubarb was known to all.

If the recipes in this Pioneer section are simple, it is because they accurately reflect the food available to pioneers. The range of supplies was limited and money to purchase them scarce. Variety depended on the skill and initiative of the homemaker.

The pioneer homemaker had little time for frills in cooking. Much of her energy was spent in sewing for the home and children, looking after the garden, feeding the farm animals, gathering fuel, and sometimes helping with the clearing itself.

It is the hope of Saskatchewan Women's Institute that these recipes will remind you of those courageous, indispensable women, the pioneers.

ROSE HIP SYRUP

Use ripe, red rose hips.

3	pounds rose hips	1.5 kg
2¼	cups sugar	625 mL

Wash rose hips and drain. Cover with water and boil for about 10 minutes until tender. Mash well and drain through a jelly bag. Cover with water again and boil 10 minutes more. Drain overnight in jelly bag.

Next morning, mix juices from both drainings; boil until you have 6 cups (1.5 L) juice. Add sugar and stir to dissolve. Boil for 5 minutes and seal in hot, sterile jars. Yield: 4 pints.

HOMEMADE YEAST CAKES

1	quart fresh buttermilk	1 L
1	package yeast	8 g
½	cup warm water	125 mL
	cornmeal	

Bring buttermilk to a boil, stirring constantly. Remove from heat; cool. Soak yeast in water. Add yeast to buttermilk and mix in cornmeal to produce a thick batter. Cover and let stand for 4 hours. Place on board in 2-tablespoon (30 mL) portions. Turn the cakes each day until they are firm and dry.

AIR BUNS

1	teaspoon sugar	5 mL
½	cup warm water	125 mL
1	package yeast	8 g
½	cup sugar	125 mL
½	cup shortening	125 mL
1	teaspoon salt	5 mL
2	tablespoons vinegar	30 mL
3½	cups warm water	875 mL
8-10	cups flour	2-2.5 L

Dissolve one teaspoon (5 mL) sugar in water; sprinkle in yeast. Let stand 10 minutes. Mix ½ cup (125 mL) sugar, shortening, salt, vinegar and water in a large bowl. Stir in yeast and flour. Knead and let rise 2 hours.

Knead again and let rise 1 hour. Knead and form into buns. Let rise and bake at 350°F (180°C) for 20 minutes. Yield: 60 rolls

BATTER BUNS

Quick and easy.

1	teaspoon sugar	5 mL
½	cup warm water	125 mL
1	package yeast	8 g
1	cup milk	250 mL
2	tablespoons butter or margarine	30 mL
2	tablespoons sugar	30 mL
1	teaspoon salt	5 mL
1	egg	1
3-3½	cups flour	750-875 mL

Dissolve sugar in water; sprinkle in yeast. Let stand 10 minutes. In saucepan combine milk and butter. Heat until butter melts, pour into large mixing bowl and cool. Stir in sugar, salt, egg and dissolved yeast. Gradually beat in flour until too stiff to stir. This can be done with a mixer — no kneading.

Let rise for 1 hour. Beat batter down vigorously. Spoon into well greased muffin tins.

Let rise another hour. Bake at 375°F (190°C) for 15 minutes. Yield: 12 buns

FLOWER POT BREAD

Temper new clay flower pots [4-inch (10 cm) or 6-inch (15 cm)] by rubbing inside and out with cooking oil. Place on cookie sheet; bake in oven at 450°F (230°C) for one hour. When ready to use for bread making, oil inside of pots again, cover the hole with a small circle of oiled paper. Never wash the pots; wipe clean with a paper towel.

2	medium potatoes	2
2	cups water	500 mL
2	teaspoons salt	10 mL
2	tablespoons sugar	30 mL
2	tablespoons shortening	30 mL
2	packages yeast	16 g
2	cups whole-wheat flour	500 mL
2½-3	cups flour	625-750 mL

Boil peeled potatoes in water until tender. Do not drain. Mash potatoes until free from lumps. Pour into large mixing bowl, add salt, sugar, shortening, cool. Sprinkle on yeast, let stand 10 minutes. Beat together well. Gradually add flours. Turn out dough on a floured baking surface. Knead well. Shape into a ball. Place in greased bowl, rotating dough to grease surface. Cover and let rise until double in bulk.

Punch down and shape into 4 loaves. Let rise again. Bake at 400°F (200°C) for 35 to 45 minutes. Yield: three 4-inch (10 cm) loaves and one 6-inch (15 cm) loaf

WHOLE WHEAT BREAD

A compact loaf of good flavor, calculated to please natural food enthusiasts.

½	teaspoon sugar	2 mL
⅓	cup warm water	75 mL
2	packages yeast	16 g
2	cups milk	500 mL
1	tablespoon margarine	15 mL
1	tablespoon salt	15 mL
½	cup honey	125 mL
5½	cups whole wheat flour	1250 mL

Dissolve sugar in water, sprinkle on yeast. Let stand 10 minutes. Heat milk to simmer, stir in margarine, salt and honey. Pour into large mixer bowl and cool. Add yeast and 3 cups (750 mL) of flour. Beat with food mixer for 8 minutes. Turn onto floured baking surface and knead in remainder of flour. Shape into ball. Place in greased bowl, rotating dough to grease surface. Cover and let rise until double in bulk.

Punch down and let rise again. Knead down, shape into 2 loaves, place in greased loaf pans and let rise until just above pans. Bake at 375°F (190°C) for 45 minutes. Yield: 2 loaves

SOURDOUGH

A "sourdough" was a prospector who of necessity learned the art of bread-making using sourdough instead of yeast. With the new interest in natural foods, sourdough bread is popular again. It also lends itself to camping and trailer living because its ingredients are staples usually carried in trailers or packsack.

Beginner cooks may not know that sourdoughs are known by a variety of names such as Monster Dough, Herman, Everlasting Yeast and Chair Dough.

Sourdough culture (without yeast):

| 1 | cup flour | 250 mL |
| 1 | cup milk | 250 mL |

Leave milk in a warm place for 24 hours. Stir in flour. Leave in warm place until it bubbles and gets sour. For a really active sourdough, cover the culture with cheesecloth and take to a warm place outdoors in order to catch yeast cells floating in the air.

Store culture in covered glass or plastic container, always stir with a wooden spoon.

To replace sourdough culture:

1½	cups sourdough culture	375 mL
1	cup milk	250 mL
1	cup flour	250 mL
¼	cup sugar	50 mL

Mix together. Do not use for 24 hours. The longer you keep and use sourdough culture, the better it gets. If you can't use the culture for a while, freeze it. When you wish to use it again, thaw the culture, then wait 24 hours or until it is bubbling well.

SOURDOUGH STARTER (with yeast)

1	package yeast	1
¼	cup sugar	50 mL
2	cups water	500 mL
2	cups flour	500 mL

Place all ingredients in 2-quart (2 L) sealer (never use a metal container). Allow to rise and recede. Cover lightly. When liquid appears on the top of the starter it is ready for use. Once it is ready, keep in a cool place and use at least every 2 days. To replace, follow instructions for sourdough culture (without yeast).

SOURDOUGH PANCAKES

2	tablespoons butter or margarine	30 mL
3	tablespoons sugar	45 mL
2	eggs	2
1	teaspoon soda	5 mL
1	cup water	250 mL
1½	cups flour	375 mL
1	teaspoon baking powder	5 mL
½	teaspoon salt	3 mL
2	tablespoons starter	30 mL

Cream butter and sugar. Add eggs, one at a time, and mix well. Dissolve soda in water and add to mixture; add flour, baking powder and salt. Stir in starter; mix well. Cook on hot griddle; grease griddle for first batch only. Yield: 16 pancakes

SOURDOUGH BISCUITS

1	cup flour	250 mL
2	teaspoons baking powder	10 mL
¼	teaspoon salt	1 mL
¼	teaspoon soda	1 mL
⅓	cup shortening	75 mL
1	cup starter	250 mL

Mix all ingredients except starter together. Add starter, stir lightly. Turn dough onto lightly-floured board and knead 8 to 10 times. Roll out ¾ inch (2 cm) thick. Cut into shapes. Bake at 400°F (200°C) for 12 to 15 minutes. Yield: 12 biscuits

SOURDOUGH SCONES

1	cup flour	250 mL
¼	teaspoon salt	1 mL
1	tablespoon baking powder	15 mL
½	teaspoon soda	2 mL
¼	cup cooking oil	60 mL
1	cup starter	250 mL

Mix and knead like bread. Roll in a circle 1¼ inch (3 cm) thick. Cut into wedges. Place on ungreased baking sheet. Bake at 425°F (220°C) for 10 to 12 minutes. Yield: 10 scones

SOURDOUGH CINNAMON BUNS

1	cup starter	250 mL
⅓	cup oil	75 mL
1	egg, beaten	1
1	cup flour	250 mL
½	teaspoon salt	2 mL
½	teaspoon soda	2 mL
2	teaspoons baking powder	10 mL
½	cup soft butter	125 mL
¾	cup brown sugar	175 mL
2	teaspoons cinnamon	10 mL
⅓	cup raisins	75 mL

Put starter in bowl, add oil and egg. Add flour, salt, soda and baking powder and mix well. Dough is quite soft. Turn out on floured board and knead slightly. Roll out into rectangle and spread with butter, sprinkle with brown sugar, cinnamon and raisins. Roll up and cut into 1-inch (2.5 cm) pieces. Place on greased baking sheet. Bake at 425°F (220°C) for 15 to 20 minutes. Yield: 12-14

SOURDOUGH CRESCENT ROLLS

Follow cinnamon bun recipe but roll into a 9-inch (22.5 cm) circle. Cut circle into 16 wedges. Roll up each wedge, starting at wide point and rolling to the center. Place on greased baking sheet. Bake at 400°F (200°C) for 10 minutes. Yield: 16 crescent rolls

SOURDOUGH BREAD

Sourdough bread takes longer to rise than ordinary bread. It is not as light, but the longer rising gives time for the development of a good flavor.

2½	cups warm water	625 mL
1	cup starter	250 mL
¼	cup melted shortening	60 mL
¼	cup sugar	60 mL
2	teaspoons salt	10 mL
3	cups flour	750 mL
1	teaspoon soda	5 mL
1	teaspoon baking powder	5 mL
3½	cups flour	875 mL

Mix well together the first 6 ingredients. Set in a warm place for 4 to 6 hours.

Add soda, baking powder and 1 cup (250 mL) flour. Beat well. Knead in remainder of flour. Shape into loaves and let rise in loaf pans. Bake at 375°F (190°C) for 35 minutes. Yield: 2 loaves

BANNOCK

This primitive sort of bread was introduced into the west by the Selkirk settlers. It has become a favorite of northern fur trappers.

2	cups flour	500 mL
1	teaspoon salt	5 mL
3	teaspoons baking powder	15 mL
¼	cup shortening	60 mL
¾	cup water	175 mL

Sift flour, baking powder and salt into bowl. Cut in shortening until mixture resembles coarse bread crumbs. Add water and mix quickly to a soft dough. Turn out on floured board, knead lightly for 30 seconds and pat into a 10-inch (25 cm) round. Cook in lightly greased frypan over medium heat until brown (about 15 minutes per side). Serve warm. Yield: One 10-inch (25 cm) bannock

CORN BREAD

Truly native to America.

2	eggs	2
½	cup sugar	125 mL
1¼	cups cream	315 mL
1	cup cornmeal	250 mL
1	cup flour	250 mL
1	tablespoon baking powder	15 mL
¼	teaspoon salt	1 mL

Beat eggs, then beat in remainder of ingredients. Pour into a hot, buttered 8 x 11 inch (20 x 28 cm) pan. Bake at 350°F (180°C) for 20 minutes. Cut in squares, serve hot with butter and syrup.

COFFEE CAKE

Bake batter:

½	cup shortening	125 mL
1	cup sugar	250 mL
¼	cup brown sugar	50 mL
2	eggs	2
2	cups flour	500 mL
2	teaspoons baking powder	10 mL
1	teaspoon baking soda	5 mL
¼	teaspoon salt	1 mL
1	teaspoon vanilla	5 mL
1	cup sour milk	250 mL

Topping:

½	cup cherries, chopped	125 mL
½	cup nuts, chopped	125 mL
¼	cup brown sugar	65 mL
1	teaspoon cinnamon	5 mL

Mix a bit of flour into topping in a bowl. Cream shortening, sugar and eggs. Add dry ingredients alternately with sour milk. Grease a 9-inch (22 cm) square pan, put in half the batter, then sprinkle well with half of the topping. Add remaining batter, then balance of the topping. Bake at 350°F (180°C) about 55 minutes.

CRUMB CAKE

2	cups flour	500 mL
1	cup sugar	250 mL
¾	cup margarine	175 mL
1	cup sour milk	250 mL
1	teaspoon soda	5 mL
1	teaspoon cloves	5 mL
1	teaspoon cinnamon	5 mL
1	egg	1
1	cup currants or raisins	250 mL

Mix flour and sugar, add butter and rub to crumbs. Set aside 1 cup (250 mL) for topping. Dissolve soda in sour milk and mix with crumbs. Blend in spices and egg. Spread in greased 8-inch (20 cm) square pan. Sprinkle with reserved crumbs. Bake at 350°F (180°C) for 35 to 45 minutes.

ALL PURPOSE READY-MIX

This will keep fresh for 2 months. Recipes using the mix follow.

9	cups flour	2.25 L
1	tablespoon salt	15 mL
⅓	cup baking powder	75 mL
2	cups shortening	500 mL

Mix dry ingredients in large bowl. With pastry blender or 2 knives cut in shortening. Store in covered container in refrigerator. Yield: 11 cups (2.75 L)

Hot biscuits:

2½	cups all purpose ready-mix	625 mL
1	egg	1
½	cup milk or cream	125 mL

Measure mix into bowl. Make a well in center and add milk and egg; stir. Turn dough out on floured baking surface; knead well 6 times. Pat or roll out and cut into shapes. Bake at 400°F (200°C) for 12 to 15 minutes. Yield: 12 medium tea biscuits

Blueberry muffins:

1	egg	1
½	cup sugar	125 mL
1	cup milk	250 mL
3	cups all purpose ready-mix	750 mL
1	cup blueberries	250 mL

In a small bowl mix egg, sugar and milk. Stir in mix and blueberries (do not overmix). Spoon into greased muffin cups. Bake at 425°F (220°C) for 20 minutes. Yield: 24 muffins

Apple pancakes:

2	eggs	2
½	cup milk	125 mL
1½	cups all purpose ready-mix	375 mL
1	tablespoon sugar	15 mL
½	cup peeled apple, chopped	125 mL

Beat egg, add milk. Gently stir in mix, sugar and apple. Cook on lightly greased griddle. Yield: 12 pancakes

BOSTON BROWN BREAD

Serve with Boston Baked Beans.

1	cup flour	250 mL
1	teaspoon baking powder	5 mL
1	teaspoon baking soda	5 mL
1	teaspoon salt	5 mL
1	cup cornmeal	250 mL
1	cup whole wheat flour	250 mL
¾	cup molasses	175 mL
2	cups buttermilk or sour milk	500 mL
1	cup raisins (optional)	250 mL

Mix all dry ingredients together. Add molasses, buttermilk and raisins; beat well. Grease and flour four large food cans. Divide batter equally into each mold. Cover tops tightly. Cook in steamer or on a rack in a deep pot containing boiling water; the water level should be considerably lower than the level of the pudding. Steam 3 hours. Turn out of mold on baking sheet; place in hot oven for a few minutes to dry the outer side of the bread. Yield: 4 loaves

NOODLES

2	eggs	2
¼	teaspoon salt	1 mL
1	cup flour	250 mL

Beat eggs until light, add salt and flour gradually. Knead until smooth and elastic. Turn out on floured baking surface and roll very thin. Using a sharp knife, cut dough in strips 2 inches (5 cm) wide. Then cut strips into fine noodles. Be certain noodles are thoroughly dry before storing in covered jar.

Cook noodles in boiling water; drain, add butter to taste or serve with tomato sauce.

CURING A HAM

2	cups salt	500 mL
2	cups sugar	500 mL
1	cup molasses	250 mL
1	teaspoon cinnamon	5 mL
1	teaspoon cloves	5 mL
1	teaspoon saltpetre	5 mL

Place ham to be cured in a large enamel pan or tub. Mix the ingredients and add enough water to cover the ham. Leave for at least 2 weeks, turning ham every day. Remove ham, rub well with spices that have settled to bottom of pan. Hang to dry.

DRY SALT CURE FOR PORK

For each 100 pounds (50 kg) of pork:

5	pounds salt	2.5 kg
3	pounds brown sugar	1.5 kg
2	ounces saltpetre	57 g
2	tablespoons black pepper	30 mL

Mix well, then rub pork once every 3 days with one third of the mixture. A week or 10 days after the last rubbing the bacon will be ready to hang. It can then be smoked. Shoulders and ham will take 6 to 7 weeks longer.

Alternate instructions

Rub the cure mixture thoroughly into hams, shoulders or bacon, especially around the bones. Put in barrel or crock, rind side down; cover with a cloth.

Let stand for 7 to 10 days, depending on temperature. Rub each piece the second time and return to the crock for another 7 to 10 days.

Repeat the process for the third time. Hang meat for a few days. Then put pieces in a cotton sack and hang by a cord in a cool place.

Bacon is just rubbed once.

The oat granary was a suitable cool storage spot for cured ham in the days of the pioneer and until the advent of modern refrigeration.

HEAD CHEESE

Have a pig's head well cleaned, brains, ears, eyes removed and the head cut into four pieces. When cutting up the meat be sure to skin the tongue and use only a small amount of the cheek part. Put in a large kettle and cover with cold water. A few well cleaned pig's feet may be added and will help to jelly the cheese. Skim the boiling mixture from time to time, until all scum is removed. Simmer until meat falls from bones.

Lift out the pieces and strain broth carefully. Cut the meat into small sections and add to the broth and simmer until mixture is fairly thick, which may take 2 to 3 hours. Season with salt and pepper. Poultry sage is well liked by some for flavoring. Pour hot mixture into bowls or sealers and keep very cold.

This makes a nice firm 'meat' jelly when cold and is easily sliced. Head cheese may be boiled up again and poured into molds for slicing.

VEGETABLE PIE

2	tablespoons fat	30 mL
½	cup onion, chopped	125 mL
1	cup carrot, sliced	250 mL
1	cup peas	250 mL
1	cup green beans	250 mL
1	cup milk	250 mL
¼	teaspoon pepper	1 mL
½	teaspoon celery seed	2 mL
1	cup mashed potatoes	250 mL
½	teaspoon salt	2 mL
¼	teaspoon pepper	1 mL
½	cup flour	125 mL
1	teaspoon baking powder	5 mL
2	tablespoons melted butter	30 mL

Melt fat, fry onion. Add vegetables, milk, pepper and celery seed. Pour into deep baking dish. Mix potatoes, salt, pepper, flour, baking powder and butter. Turn onto floured baking surface and roll big enough to cover baking dish. Bake at 350°F (180°C) for 30 minutes. Yield: 6 servings

PORK AND BEANS

2½	cups beans	625 mL
4	cups water	1 L
1	teaspoon baking soda	5 mL
1	cup salt pork, chopped	250 mL
1	cup onion, chopped	250 mL
1	cup catsup	250 mL
½	cup brown sugar	125 mL
¼	cup molasses	65 mL
1	tablespoon salt	15 mL
½	teaspoon pepper	2 mL
1	teaspoon dry mustard	5 mL

Soak beans in water overnight.

Drain, cover with fresh water, add baking soda and simmer until skins split. Drain and place beans in large casserole. Mix remaining ingredients together and pour over beans. Cover and bake at 300°F (150°C) for 3 hours. Add a small amount of water from time to time so that beans do not become dry. Yield: 6 servings

BOILED-RAISIN CAKE

A very tender, moist cake.

1	cup raisins	250 mL
½	cup butter	125 mL
¾	cup sugar	175 mL
1	egg	1
1¾	cup flour	425 mL
½	teaspoon nutmeg	2 mL
1	teaspoon cinnamon	5 mL
¼	teaspoon salt	1 mL
1½	teaspoon cocoa	7 mL
1	teaspoon baking soda	5 mL
¾	cup raisin water	175 mL

Put raisins in saucepan, cover with water and simmer 10 minutes. Cream butter and sugar, add egg and beat. Sift flour, spices, salt and cocoa. Add dry ingredients to the creamed mixture alternately with soda mixed into raisin water. If raisins have soaked up water, make total up to ¾ cup or 175 mL. Pour into 8-inch (20 cm) square pan. Bake at 300°F (150°C) for 40 minutes. Watch closely as cake burns easily.

VANILLA SAUCE

2	eggs	2
2	cups icing sugar	500 mL
½	cup hot milk	125 mL
¼	teaspoon salt	1 mL
1	teaspoon vanilla	5 mL

Beat eggs until fluffy. Add icing sugar to eggs alternately with milk. Add salt and vanilla. Flavor with cognac if desired. Yield: 2½ cups

GRANNIE CHAPLIN'S ICING

Use to frost Boiled Raisin Cake.

1½	cups brown sugar	375 mL
½	cup milk	125 mL
¼	teaspoon salt	1 mL
4	tablespoons butter	60 mL
½	teaspoon vanilla	2 mL

Mix brown sugar, milk and salt in heavy saucepan. Cook over medium heat until mixture reaches soft-ball stage, 236°F (115°C). Add butter and cool. Add vanilla and beat until thick. Yield: frosting for an 8-inch (20 cm) cake

OLD-FASHIONED BOSTON CREAM PIE

¾	cup brown sugar	175 mL
2	tablespoons flour	30 mL
¼	teaspoon nutmeg	1 mL
¼	teaspoon salt	1 mL
1½	cups creamilk	375 mL
1	teaspoon vanilla	5 mL
1	8-inch pie shell, unbaked	20 cm

Mix sugar, flour, nutmeg and salt in heavy saucepan; stir in cream. Cook slowly over low heat until mixture thickens. Stir in vanilla. Pour into pie shell. Bake at 425°F (220°C) for 10 minutes. Reduce temperature to 350°F (180°C) and bake 30 minutes more. Chill thoroughly. Top with whipped cream and toasted coconut. Yield: 6 servings.

CARROT PIE

2	eggs	2
2	cups cooked, mashed carrots	500 mL
¾	cup sugar	175 mL
1	teaspoon cinnamon	5 mL
½	teaspoon nutmeg	2 mL
½	teaspoon ginger	2 mL
¼	teaspoon salt	1 mL
½	cup milk	125 mL
1	9-inch pie shell, unbaked	22.5 cm

Beat eggs lightly. Add carrots, sugar, cinnamon, nutmeg, ginger and salt. Beat to blend well; stir in milk. Pour into pie shell. Bake at 400°F (200°C) for 10 minutes. Reduce temperature to 350°F (180°C) and continue baking for 30 minutes until a knife inserted comes out clean. Garnish with whipped cream. Yield: 6 servings

RAISIN PIE

1	cup raisins	250 mL
6 or 8	dates, chopped fine	6-8
2	tablespoons flour	30 mL
1	cup brown sugar	250 mL
¼	teaspoon cinnamon	1 mL
1	tablespoon vinegar	15 mL
1	teaspoon butter	5 mL
¼	teaspoon salt	1 mL
1½	cups water	375 mL

Mix all ingredients in heavy saucepan. Cook over low heat, stirring often, for about 15 minutes. Cool. Pour into pastry-lined, 8-inch (20 cm) pie plate. Cover with top crust; seal edges. Bake at 450°F (230°C) for 10 minutes. Reduce temperature to 350°F (180°C) and bake 30 minutes more. Yield: 6 servings

SASKATOON PIE

4	cups fresh Saskatoons	1 L
½	cup sugar mixed with	125 mL
2	tablespoons minute tapioca or flour	30 mL
¼	teaspoon salt	1 mL
1	teaspoon almond flavoring or 1 teaspoon lemon juice	5 mL
1	teaspoon butter	5 mL

Line pie pan with pastry. Add the Saskatoon mixture. Put on top crust.

Bake ½ hour at 450°F (230°C) for cooked berries or 15 minutes at 450°F (230°C) and ½ hour at 375°F (190°C) for uncooked berries.

PAPER BAG APPLE PIE

1	9-inch pie shell, unbaked	22.5 cm
7	cups baking apples	1.75 L
½	cup sugar	125 mL
2	tablespoons flour	30 mL
1	teaspoon nutmeg	5 mL
2	tablespoons lemon juice	30 mL
½	cup sugar	125 mL
½	cup flour	125 mL
½	cup margarine	125 mL

Core and quarter apples; cut each quarter in half crosswise to make chunks. Combine sugar, flour and nutmeg and sprinkle over apples. Spoon into pastry shell. Drizzle with lemon juice. Mix remaining sugar, flour and margarine until crumbly. Spread over apples to cover top. Slide pie into heavy brown paper bag large enough to cover pie loosely. Fold open end over twice and fasten with paper clips. Place on cookie sheet to avoid burning. Bake at 425°F (220°C) for 1 hour. Split bag open to remove pie, cool on wire rack. Serve plain, with cheese or with ice cream. Yield: 6 servings

SCOTCH OATCAKES

Serve with cheese or butter and marmalade for afternoon tea.

3	cups rolled oats	750 mL
3	cups flour	750 mL
1	cup sugar	250 mL
2	teaspoons salt	10 mL
2	cups shortening	500 mL
4-5	tablespoons water	60-75 mL

Combine oats, flour, sugar and salt. Cut in shortening until mixture resembles fine crumbs. Add enough water to form a dough that can be easily rolled. Turn out on floured baking surface. Roll dough thin and cut in 2-inch (5 cm) squares. Bake at 350°F (180°C) for 15 minutes until browned. Yield: 60 oatcakes

OLD FASHIONED APPLE ROLL-UP

2½	cups flour	625 mL
½	teaspoon salt	2 mL
¾	cup sugar	175 mL
½	cup margarine	125 mL
2	eggs	2
⅓	cup milk	75 mL
3	cups apples, chopped	750 mL
1	tablespoon lemon juice	15 mL
½	cup nuts, chopped	125 mL
2	tablespoons sugar	30 mL
½	teaspoon cinnamon	2 mL
½	cup raisins (optional)	125 mL

Sift together flour, salt and sugar in large bowl. Cut in margarine. Beat milk and eggs. Remove 2 tablespoonfuls (30 mL) and set aside. Add remainder to flour mixture and blend well. Form into ball, cover and chill one hour.

Combine apples, lemon juice, nuts, sugar, cinnamon and raisins for filling. Turn dough out on floured baking surface and roll dough very thin. Sprinkle filling over the dough, roll up. Seal the edges with milk and egg mixture. Bake on greased baking sheet at 400°F (200°C) for 30 minutes or until golden brown. Yield: 10 to 12 servings

SOAP

4	cups soft water	1 L
4	tablespoons ammonia	60 mL
4	tablespoons Borax	60 mL
1	9½-ounce can lye	270 gm
8	cups fat	2 L

Put lye in cold water with borax and ammonia, then stir. Melt grease to 110°F (40°C). Cool lye to 90°F (35°C). Put lye into fat, stir until like honey. Pour into wooden flats lined with thin cotton, cool; cut in squares.

HOMEMADE SOAP

1	9½-ounce can lye flakes	270 gm
10	cups fat	2.5 L
½	cup borax	125 mL
½	cup sugar	125 mL
3	pints cold water	1.5 L
1	tablespoon ammonia	15 mL
1	dessertspoon baking soda	10 mL

Dissolve lye in 2 pints (1 L) cold water. Let cool to 100°F (38°C). Into small dish put remaining pint (500 mL) of water, ammonia, borax, sugar and baking soda. Warm fat to 95°F (36°C). Very gradually add lye mixture in thin stream to the fat, stirring only slowly with wooden spoon. Then add contents of small dish, stirring for half an hour until thick (like honey). Pour into a wooden box to set.

FESTIVE
FOODS

"**T**O BE a good cook means the economy of great-grandmothers and the science of modern chemists. It means English thoroughness, French art and Arabian hospitality. It means, in fine, that you are to see that everyone has something nice to eat."

John Ruskin

When prairie families gather for a festive occasion, there is always something particularly nice for everyone to eat. In a province where winter can sometimes prevail for six months and the wind puts an edge to appetite, the appreciation of fine food is the keener.

Lucky the person who can manage the usual Christmas feast with roast turkey and stuffing, vegetables of all kinds and mince pie and then later in January go on to celebrate with a Ukrainian family the beautiful Christmas evening meal of twelve Lenten dishes.

Community festivals may be the observance of customs so old that their origins are lost in the mists of time, like the feast to celebrate taking off the harvest. In many prairie communities there is still a fowl supper in the fall, with everyone helping by donating food or labor and rejoicing when the proceeds go to some worthy cause. The pattern of the fowl supper with platters of turkey, bowls of peas and carrots, mashed turnip, jellied salads and an array of pies bespeak the abundance of the year. If the crop of Saskatoons has been good, there will be Saskatoon pie; almost everyone will be able to provide pumpkin pie and butter tarts. More recent additions to the array of fowl supper foods are the cabbage roll and bean salad.

The community feasts provoke an outpouring of fine food and good fellowship, and enhance the stability of community life and the unity of families, a value highly prized by Saskatchewan Women's Institute. A more casual way of entertaining, the buffet, or for those who risk an unplanned menu, the pot luck supper, may produce an assortment of main course casseroles ranging from Italian pastas to Chinese cookery, salads of all kinds, and an overwhelming variety of gorgeous layered desserts.

It is some of these culinary achievements that we share with you.

FESTIVE PUNCH

2	48-ounce cans orange juice	2.75	L
2	48-ounce cans grapefruit juice	2.75	L
2	48-ounce cans pineapple juice	2.75	L
1	6½-ounce can frozen lemonade	178	mL
3¼	cups of cold water	800	mL
2	26-ounce bottles ginger ale	1.5	L
2	pints lime sherbet	1	L

Combine orange, grapefruit and pineapple juices, lemonade and water. Stir thoroughly and chill.

Immediately before serving add ginger ale and sherbet. Stir once again until the sherbet is dissolved. Ice cubes may be added if desired. Yield: 30 servings

PARTY PUNCH

1	pound cranberries	454	g
4	cups water	1	L
1½	cups sugar	375	mL
3	cups hot tea	750	mL
3	cups orange juice	750	mL
1	cup lemon juice	250	mL
1	quart iced water	1	L
1	quart ginger ale	1	L
	orange and lemon slices		

Simmer cranberries in water until the skins burst. Strain or drip through jelly bag. Combine with sugar and tea, stir until sugar dissolves. Cool.

Add orange and lemon juice and iced water. Pour over ice cubes in large bowl, add ginger ale and garnish with orange and lemon slices. Yield: 30 punch-cups.

SEAFOOD COCKTAIL SAUCE

¾	cup catsup	175	mL
½	teaspoon seasoned salt	2	mL
2	tablespoons prepared horseradish	30	mL
3	tablespoons lemon juice	45	mL
	few drops Tabasco sauce		

Combine all ingredients and chill thoroughly.

SHRIMP COCKTAIL

Clean cooked shrimp, removing black line from back, chill.

Mix in finely chopped celery; season. For each serving, place 4 to 6 shrimps in a lettuce-lined cocktail cup set in ice. Add cocktail sauce, garnish with lemon wedge.

PIGS IN BLANKETS

1	pound cocktail sausages	.5 kg
1¾	cup flour	425 mL
4	teaspoons baking powder	20 mL
½	teaspoon salt	2 mL
⅓	cup shortening	75 mL
¾	cup milk	175 mL
	mustard relish	

Parboil cocktail sausages, drain

Measure flour, baking powder and salt into mixing bowl; cut in shortening with blender or two knives. Add milk and stir with a fork until moistened. Turn out onto lightly–floured surface and knead gently. Roll into rectangle. Cut into 2-inch (5 cm) squares. Spread dough with mustard relish. Place a cooked sausage on corner end of square of dough; roll up diagonally. Place on baking sheet; bake at 450°F (230°C) for 15 minutes. Yield: 18 servings.

LIVER PÂTÉ

1	envelope gelatine	7 g
¾	cup cold water	175 mL
1	cup liver sausage	250 mL
⅓	cup salad dressing	75 mL
⅓	cup sour cream	75 mL
1½	tablespoons onion, minced	25 mL
¾	teaspoon Worcestershire sauce	3 mL

Soften gelatine in cold water for 5 minutes. Dissolve over low heat; cool. Add liver sausage, salad dressing, sour cream, minced onion and Worcestershire sauce. Blend well (a food blender makes a smooth product). Pour into greased mold.

Chill, serve on crackers.

APRICOT MOUSSE SALAD

2	14-ounce cans apricot halves	796 mL
1	3-ounce package lemon jelly powder	85 g
1	3-ounce package orange jelly powder	85 g
¾	cup cold water	175 mL
⅔	cup salad dressing	150 mL
⅓	cup ginger ale	75 mL
1	8-ounce package cream cheese	227 g
2	egg whites	2
¼	cup sugar	65 mL

Drain juice from apricots. Add sufficient water to make 2 cups (500 mL). Heat to boiling, stir in jelly powders. Add cold water. Blend salad dressing and ginger ale; mix with cream cheese. Stir into fruit gelatine and chill. Chop 1½ cups (375 mL) of apricots. Beat egg whites, gradually adding sugar. Continue beating until eggs form stiff peaks. Fold apricots and egg whites into gelatine mixture. Pour into mold and chill until firm. Garnish with remaining apricots.

24-HOUR SALAD

2	cups pineapple tidbits, drained	500 mL
2	cups green grapes	500 mL
2	cups orange segments, drained	500 mL
2	cups miniature marshmallows	500 mL
2	eggs, beaten	2
¼	cup vinegar	50 mL
4	tablespoons sugar	50 mL
2	tablespoons butter	30 mL
1	cup whipping cream	250 mL

Mix pineapple, grapes, orange segments and marshmallows. Chill.

In the top of a double boiler combine eggs with sugar and vinegar. Cook over hot water until thick. Add butter and cool. Whip cream and fold into egg mixture. Pour over fruit and marshmallows, combine gently. Chill for 24 hours. Yield: 10 servings.

FRUIT SALAD DRESSING

3	eggs, beaten	3
1	cup sugar	250 mL
¼	cup lemon juice	65 mL
1½	cups pineapple juice	375 mL
1	tablespoon butter	15 mL
1	cup whipping cream	250 mL

Combine eggs, sugar, juices in top of double boiler. Cook until thickened, stirring constantly. Cool.

When ready to use, whip cream, fold into egg mixture. Use on any mixed, fresh fruit salad. Yield: 3 cups (750 mL).

DELICIOUS LAYER SALAD

First layer:

1	3-ounce package lime jelly powder	85 g
1	cup boiling water	250 mL
1	cup crushed pineapple, drained	250 mL

Second layer:

1	3-ounce package lemon jelly powder	85 g
1	cup boiling water	250 mL
1	cup cottage cheese	250 mL
1	cup whipping cream	250 mL

Third layer:

1	3-ounce package cherry jelly powder	85 g
1¾	cups boiling water	425 mL
1	cup fruit	250 mL

Dissolve lime jelly powder in boiling water; when partially set add pineapple and pour into 9 x 13 inch (22 x 33 cm) pan. Let partially set.

Dissolve lemon jelly powder in boiling water. Whip cream and mix with cottage cheese. When partially set, fold in cheese mixture. Pour over first layer.

Dissolve cherry jelly powder in boiling water. When partially set, fold in fruit. Pour over second layer. Chill until firm. Cut into squares. Yield: 20 servings.

SOUR CREAM SALAD

1	cup sour cream (or whipped sweet cream)	250 mL
1	cup mandarin orange segments, drained	250 mL
1	cup fruit salad, drained	250 mL
1	cup crushed pineapple, drained	250 mL
1 ½	cups miniature marshmallows	375 mL
¼	cup coconut	65 mL

Mix all together and chill over night in refrigerator. Yield: 6 servings.

PINEAPPLE AND CARROT SALAD

2	3-ounce packages lemon jelly powder	170 g
3	cups boiling water	750 mL
5	tablespoons vinegar	75 mL
1	19-ounce can crushed pineapple	520 mL
1	cup carrots, shredded	250 mL

Dissolve jelly powders in hot water, add vinegar. Let chill until slightly thickened. Add pineapple with juice and carrots. Pour into large flat pan. Chill.

To serve, cut in squares and place on lettuce. Garnish with salad dressing and olives.

SHRIMP SALAD

2	cups tomato juice	500 mL
2	tablespoons vinegar	30 mL
1	teaspoon salt	5 mL
1	tablespoon onion, grated	15 mL
1	3-ounce package lemon jelly powder	85 g
1	4 ounce can shrimp	113 g
½	cup celery, chopped	125 mL

Heat tomato juice, vinegar, salt and onion to boiling. Pour in jelly powder, heat until dissolved. When partially set, fold in shrimp and celery. Yield: 10 servings.

RASPBERRY RING WITH CREAMY FRUIT

1	6-ounce package raspberry jelly powder	170 g
2	cups boiling water	500 mL
1	pint raspberry sherbet	500 mL

Dissolve jelly powder in boiling water. Stir in raspberry sherbet. Pour into 4-cup (1L) ring mold. Chill.

Unmold and fill center with Sour Cream Salad (see recipe p. 73). Yield: 10 servings.

TUTTI-FRUTTI WREATH

2	teaspoons sugar	10 mL
½	cup warm water	125 mL
2	packages yeast	16 g
¾	cup milk	175 mL
6	tablespoons butter	90 mL
⅔	cup sugar	150 mL
1¼	teaspoon salt	6 mL
3	eggs	3
5	cups flour	1.25 L
½	cup mixed peel	125 mL
1	cup seedless raisins	250 mL
½	cup dates	125 mL
2	tablespoons butter	30 mL
2	cups icing sugar	500 mL
¼	teaspoon salt	1 mL
¼	cup milk	50 mL
½	teaspoon vanilla	2 mL

Dissolve sugar in warm water in large bowl. Sprinkle on yeast. Let stand 10 minutes, then stir well. In saucepan scald milk, stir in butter, sugar and salt. Add to yeast mixture along with eggs and some of the flour. Beat until smooth. Add remainder of flour. Turn out on a lightly-floured board and knead until smooth and elastic. Place in greased bowl.

Let rise until double in bulk.

Combine peel, raisins and dates, set aside. Punch dough down, turn out on lightly floured board. Divide into 2 portions.

Roll 1 portion into 12 x 18 (30 x 45 cm) rectangle. Brush with butter, spread with half the peel mixture. Starting at long end, roll up jelly-roll fashion. Seal long outer edge. Place seam-side down on greased baking sheet, shape into ring, join ends. Brush surface with butter or margarine. With scissors cut through ring to within 1 inch (2.5 cm) of inner edge, making cuts about 1 inch apart. Slightly twist each cut piece so that slices fan out and overlap each other. Repeat with remaining dough. Cover. Let rise 45 minutes.

Bake at 350°F (180°C) for 30 to 35 minutes. Let stand a few minutes. Blend icing sugar, salt, milk and vanilla; and beat to a smooth paste. Drizzle on hot wreath.

CRANBERRY BREAD

2	cups flour	500 mL
¾	cup sugar	175 mL
2	teaspoons baking powder	10 mL
½	teaspoon baking soda	2 mL
1	teaspoon salt	5 mL
½	cup shortening	125 mL
¾	cup orange juice	175 mL
1	tablespoon grated orange rind	15 mL
2	eggs, well beaten	2
1	cup cranberries, chopped	250 mL
½	cup green glace cherries, chopped (optional)	125 mL

Sift dry ingredients together. Sprinkle cranberries and cherries with a little of this mixture. Rub in shortening. Fold in orange juice, orange rind, and eggs. Mix in chopped cranberries and cherries, being careful not to over-mix or the texture will be spoiled. Spoon into a well–greased 1½-quart (1.5 L) casserole. Bake at 350°F (180°C) for about 1 hour. Cool in casserole for 10 minutes, then remove.

LEMON BREAD

1½	cups flour	375 mL
½	teaspoon salt	2 mL
1	teaspoon baking powder	5 mL
½	cup shortening	125 mL
1	cup sugar	250 mL
2	tablespoons orange rind, grated	30 mL
2	teaspoons lemon rind, grated	10 mL
2	eggs, beaten	2
½	cup milk	125 mL
2	tablespoons lemon juice	30 mL
½	cup icing sugar	125 mL

Sift dry ingredients together. Add milk to beaten eggs. Cream shortening, add sugar and rind. Add dry ingredients alternately with milk. Turn into greased loaf pan 5 x 9 inches (12 x 22 cm). Bake at 350°F (180°C) for 45 to 60 minutes.

Mix lemon juice and icing sugar. Pour over top of cake when it is still hot. Yield: 1 loaf.

POPOVERS

2	tablespoons beef dripping	30 mL
1	cup flour	250 mL
½	teaspoon salt	2 mL
2	eggs	2
1	cup milk	250 mL

Preheat oven to 425°F (220°C). Pour ½ teaspoon (2 mL) beef dripping into 8 medium-sized muffin pans. Keep warm in oven.

Mix flour and salt. Mix milk, eggs, remainder of fat; beat together. Add flour mixture and beat 2 minutes. Pour into pans. Bake 20 minutes, serve immediately. Yield: 8 popovers.

Yorkshire Pudding:
Use 8-inch (20 cm) square pan and bake for 35 minutes.

To keep popovers for reheating, slit top and allow steam to escape. Turn off oven and leave popovers for 20 minutes more. Cool in pan and reheat before serving.

PARTY SANDWICH LOAF

1	loaf unsliced bread	1
½	cup butter, softened	125 mL
½	cup each of 4 sandwich fillings	125 mL each
3	4-ounce packages cream cheese	339 mL
¼	cup creamilk	65 mL
	olive slices	

Remove crust from bread and cut lengthwise into 5 equal long slices. Prepare fillings so that they are fairly moist. Soften cream cheese with creamilk.

Butter each slice and spread with filling. Place one slice on top of the other to form a loaf. Remove excess filling. Wrap tightly in damp cloth. Place in refrigerator for 2 hours.

Cover with softened cream cheese all sides, decorate with olive slices.

Refrigerate again. Cut into slices. Yield: 10 to 12 slices

BRUNCH CASSEROLE

16-20	slices bread	16-20
8-10	slices ham or back bacon	8-10
8-10	slices cheese	8-10
6	eggs	6
½	teaspoon salt	2 mL
1	teaspoon Worcestershire sauce	5 mL
1	teaspoon dry mustard	5 mL
3	cups milk	750 mL
¼	teaspoon cayenne	1 mL
¼	teaspoon pepper	1 mL
¼	cup onion, chopped	65 mL
¼	cup green peppers, chopped	65 mL
½	cup butter, melted	125 mL
1	cup potato chips, crushed	250 mL

Remove crusts from bread. Arrange 8 to 10 slices to cover 9 x 13 inch (22 x 33 cm) buttered pan. Place a slice of ham and cheese on each slice of bread. Top with remaining bread.

Beat eggs, add salt, Worcestershire sauce, mustard, milk, cayenne, and pepper. Stir in onion and green pepper. Pour over bread mixture.

Refrigerate overnight.

Before baking pour over butter, top with potato chips. Bake at 350°F (180°C) for 1 hour. Yield 8 to 10 servings

SWEET AND SOUR MEATBALLS

1½	pounds ground beef	.75 kg
1½	teaspoons salt	7 mL
1	cup rolled oats	250 mL
½	teaspoon pepper	2 mL
1	egg, beaten	1
¼	teaspoon garlic salt	1 mL
¾	cup sugar	185 mL
2	tablespoons soya sauce	30 mL
2	tablespoons flour	30 mL
¼	teaspoon salt	1 mL
¼	cup vinegar	65 mL
2	cups boiling water	500 mL

Mix ground beef with salt, rolled oats and pepper. Add egg and garlic salt. Form into 1-inch (2.5 cm) balls; fry until brown. Drain off fat.

Mix sugar, soya, flour, salt, vinegar and boiling water together; simmer for 10 minutes. Pour over meatballs; simmer 20 minutes longer.

CHICKEN CASSEROLE

1	frying chicken	1.5 kg
¼	teaspoon marjoram	1 mL
1	19-ounce can mushroom soup	540 mL
½	cup milk	125 mL
¼	teaspoon nutmeg	1 mL
3	cups bread crumbs	750 mL
⅓	cup margarine, melted	75 mL
½	cup white wine	125 mL
¼	cup almonds, slivered	65 mL

Cut chicken in serving-sized portions. Place in shallow baking dish. Sprinkle with marjoram. Combine soup, milk and nutmeg; mix smooth with egg beater. Pour over chicken. Bake at 325°F (160°C) for 2 hours.

Combine bread crumbs and margarine; sprinkle over chicken. Pour over wine; sprinkle on almonds. Return to oven for 10 minutes. Yield: 4 servings

HOLIDAY CHICKEN À LA KING

½	cup butter	125 mL
½	cup onion, finely-diced	125 mL
½	cup celery, chopped	125 mL
½	cup green pepper, chopped	125 mL
¼	cup flour	65 mL
1½	teaspoons seasoned salt	7 mL
⅛	teaspoon pepper	.5 mL
1	10-ounce can cream of mushroom soup	284 mL
3	cups milk	750 mL
2	5-ounce cans small oysters, drained	284 mL
1	10-ounce can mushrooms, drained	284 mL
3	cups cooked chicken, diced	750 mL
¼	cup pimento, chopped	65 mL

Melt butter in large saucepan. Sauté onions, celery and green peppers until tender; blend in flour, salt and pepper. Combine soup and milk; very gradually stir into flour mixture. Cook over medium heat stirring constantly, until smoothly thickened and mixture comes to a boil. Add remaining ingredients. Cover and cook over low heat about 15 minutes.

Serve over rice, noodles or puff pastry shells. Yield: 10 servings

TIJUANA CHICKEN

1	frying chicken	1.5 - 2 kg
¼	cup flour	65 mL
1	teaspoon salt	5 mL
½	teaspoon pepper	2 mL
2	tablespoons cooking oil	30 mL
½	cup onion, chopped	125 mL
½	cup green pepper, diced	125 mL
½	cup red pepper, diced	125 mL
1	28-ounce can tomatoes	796 mL
2	teaspoons chili powder	10 mL

Cut chicken into serving-sized portions. Roll chicken in flour, seasoned with salt and pepper; brown in oil. Remove chicken from pan; add onion and peppers and sauté until tender. Add tomatoes and chili and simmer. Place chicken in roasting pan, pour over sauce. Cover and bake at 325°F (160°C) for 1½ hours.

Serve with rice. Yield: 4 to 6 servings

TUNA CASHEW CASSEROLE

1	6-ounce package chow mein noodles	170 g
1	19-ounce can cream of mushroom soup	540 mL
1	10-ounce can mushrooms	284 mL
3	7-ounce cans solid white tuna	594 g
1	cup cashews	250 mL
2	cups celery, diced	500 mL
¼	cup onion, minced	65 mL
¼	teaspoon salt	1 mL
¼	teaspoon pepper	1 mL
2¼	cups water	575 mL

Reserve half the noodles. Mix remaining ingredients; pour into large greased casserole. Bake at 350°F (180°C) for 30 minutes. Add remaining noodles and bake 10 minutes more. Yield: 14 to 16 servings.

WILD-RICE STUFFING FOR DUCK

½	cup wild rice	125 mL
1	quart boiling water	1 L
1	10-ounce can mushrooms	284 mL
½	cup onion, minced	125 mL
½	cup celery, chopped	125 mL
2	tablespoons fat	30 mL
½	teaspoon salt	2 mL
¼	teaspoon pepper	1 mL
½	teaspoon sage	2 mL
2	egg yolks, beaten	2

Soak wild rice overnight.

Drain, cook rice in boiling water for about 20 minutes; drain. Fry mushrooms, onion and celery in fat; add to rice. Add salt, pepper and sage and mix well. Blend in egg yolks. Spoon mixture into prepared duck. Yield: stuffing for 2 ducks

DARK FRUIT CAKE

1	pound butter	500 mL
2	cups sugar	500 mL
6	eggs	6
2	tablespoons molasses	30 mL
1	cup thick cream	250 mL
2	teaspoons vanilla	10 mL
1	teaspoon rum or brandy	5 mL
2	teaspoons baking powder	10 mL
1	teaspoon cinnamon	5 mL
1	teaspoon nutmeg	5 mL
½	teaspoon cloves	2 mL
2	tablespoons lemon juice	30 mL
3	cups flour	750 mL
2	pounds raisins	1000 mL
½	pound mixed peel	250 mL
1	pound mixed fruit	500 mL
1	pound cherries (red & green)	500 mL
2	pineapple rings	2
½	pound blanched almonds	550 mL

Preheat oven to 250°F (120°C). Dredge fruit with 1 cup (250 ml) flour. Cream sugar and butter, add eggs one at a time, lemon juice and molasses, cream and flavoring. Beat well. Add remaining 2 cups (500 mL) flour, baking powder and spices. Add fruit and mix well. Pour into 4 lined pans. (22 cm x 12 cm x 7 cm) and bake at 250°F (120°C) for 3½ to 4 hours.

ITALIAN FRUIT CAKE

3	cups white sugar	750 mL
2	cups butter	500 mL
10	eggs	10
1	cup orange juice	250 mL
5	cups flour	1250 mL
½	teaspoon salt	2 mL
2	pounds bleached raisins	1000 mL
1	pound mixed peel	500 mL
1	pound glazed cherries	500 mL
½	pound glazed pineapple	250 mL
½	pound blanched almonds, rolled fine	550 mL
½	pound brazil nuts, rolled fine	550 mL

Cream butter and sugar. Add unbeaten eggs one at a time beating thoroughly after each addition. Measure flour, sift and measure again. Add half alternately with orange juice, dredging fruit with remaining half. Add fruit and nuts. Bake in greased lined pans for 3 to 4 hours at 300°F (150°C). Place open pan of water in oven for moisture.

GOLDEN WEST FRUIT CAKE

An exceptionally fruity cake of fine flavor.

1	cup dried apricots	250 mL
2	cups dark raisins	500 mL
2	cups golden raisins	500 mL
8	ounces almonds, sliced	550 mL
8	ounces candied cherries, halved	250 mL
16	ounces mixed candied fruit and peel, diced	500 mL
12	ounces candied pineapple, diced	375 mL
1¼	cups shortening	300 mL
1¼	cups liquid honey	300 mL
6	eggs	6
2½	cups flour	625 mL
1	teaspoon baking powder	5 mL
1¼	teaspoons salt	6 mL
1	teaspoon cinnamon	5 mL
½	teaspoon cloves	2 mL

Preheat oven to 250°F (120°C). Line a greased 25 cm tube pan with two thicknesses of greased brown paper and one of greased wax paper. Cover apricots with boiling water, let stand 5 minutes. Drain and using scissors, cut apricots in slices. Combine apricots, raisins, nuts, cherries, candied fruit and peels mix thoroughly. Blend shortening and honey, beat in eggs, one at a time. Sift together flour, baking powder, salt and spices. Blend into batter. Stir in fruits and nuts, mixing well. Spoon into prepared pan. Bake in very slow oven with shallow pan of hot water on floor of oven for about 4 hours. Makes 1 tube cake about 7½ pounds.

NEW YEAR YULE LOG

6	tablespoons sifted flour	90 mL
6	tablespoons cocoa	90 mL
½	teaspoon baking powder	3 mL
¼	teaspoon salt	1 mL
¾	cup sugar	175 mL
4	egg whites, beaten	4
4	egg yolks, well beaten	4
1	teaspoon vanilla	5 mL
	icing sugar	
	7-minute frosting	
	chocolate icing	

Line an 8 x 13 inch (20 x 30 cm) pan with greased paper. Sift flour once, measure, add cocoa, baking powder and salt. Sift together 3 times. Beat sugar into egg whites, a small amount at a time. Add egg yolk and vanilla. Fold in flour gradually, pour into pan. Bake at 400°F (200°C) for 13 minutes.

Turn out at once on a cloth, covered with icing sugar. Remove paper from cake. Quickly cut off crisp edges of cake. Spread 7-minute frosting over cake; roll up cake and wrap in cloth. When cool, cover with chocolate icing. Yield: 12 servings

ANGEL COOKIES

1	cup butter	250 mL
½	cup white sugar	125 mL
½	cup brown sugar	125 mL
1	egg	1
2	cups flour	500 mL
1	teaspoon soda	5 mL
1	teaspoon cream of tartar	5 mL
1	teaspoon vanilla	5 mL
	pinch of salt	

Cream the butter, add sugars and cream until light and fluffy. Add egg and stir in flour, soda, cream of tartar, vanilla and salt. Roll into balls and flatten with a fork. Bake on ungreased baking sheet at 375°F (190°C) for 10 to 12 minutes.

ALMOND CHERRY BALLS

1	cup butter	250 mL
¼	cup icing sugar	65 mL
2	cups flour	500 mL
1	cup almonds, ground	250 mL
1	teaspoon vanilla	5 mL
18	maraschino cherries	18

Cream butter with sugar until fluffy. Add flour, almonds and vanilla. Take a small amount of dough, form it into a ball with a cherry in the center. Place on greased baking sheet. Bake at 325°F (160°C) for 25 to 35 minutes. Remove from oven and roll in icing sugar while still warm. Yield: 18 cookies

MEXICAN WEDDING CAKE

1	cup butter	250 mL
5	tablespoons icing sugar	75 mL
2	cups flour	500 mL
½	teaspoon salt	2 mL
1	cup pecans, chopped	250 mL
1	teaspoon vanilla	5 mL

Cream butter and sugar together. Add flour, salt, pecans and vanilla. Mix well. Knead on floured baking surface. Divide to make two 1 x 10-inch (2.5 x 25 cm) rolls. Chill.

Cut into ¾-inch (2 cm) slices. Bake at 350°F (180°C) for 20 minutes. As soon as they come from the oven, roll in icing sugar. Yield: 26 slices

WHIPPED SHORTBREAD

1	cup margarine	250 mL
¼	cup cornstarch	65 mL
½	cup icing sugar	125 mL
1½	cups flour	375 mL

Place all ingredients in a mixing bowl. Beat 10 minutes with electric mixer. Drop by spoonfuls onto cookie sheet. Bake at 325°F (160°C) for 10 minutes. Yield: 48 cookies

CONFETTI SPECIAL

1	6-ounce package butterscotch chips	175 mL
¼	cup butter	75 mL
½	cup peanut butter	125 mL
2	cups colored miniature marshmallows	500 mL

Melt chips in double boiler. Stir in butter, peanut butter and marshmallows. Spread in greased 8-inch (20 cm) square pan. Yield: 32 bars

CHOCOLATE MARSHMALLOW ROLL

2	squares semi-sweet chocolate	2
2	tablespoons butter	30 mL
½	cup walnuts	125 mL
1	egg, beaten	1
1	cup icing sugar	250 mL
1	cup colored miniature marshmallows	250 mL
½	cup coconut	125 mL
½	cup graham-wafer crumbs	125 mL

Melt chocolate and butter in double boiler, add walnuts. Mix together rest of ingredients and add chocolate mixture. Roll in waxed paper and refrigerate. Slice and serve.

CHEESE WAFERS

1	cup margarine	250 mL
2	cups old cheddar cheese, grated	500 mL
2	cups rice krispies	500 mL
2	cups flour	500 mL
½	teaspoon garlic salt	2 mL

Cream margarine, blend in cheese. Stir in dry ingredients. Roll into balls and flatten. Bake at 350°F (180°C) for 20 minutes. Store in air tight container or freeze.

PEPPER NUT COOKIES

1½	cups butter	375 mL
2	cups sugar	500 mL
2	eggs, beaten	2
1½	cups syrup	375 mL
1	cup sour cream	250 mL
1½	teaspoon soda	7 mL
½	teaspoon pepper	2 mL
½	teaspoon cinnamon	2 mL
½	teaspoon cloves	2 mL
½	teaspoon nutmeg	2 mL
½	teaspoon ginger	2 mL
½	teaspoon allspice	2 mL
8	cups flour	2 L

Cream together the butter and sugar. Add eggs, syrup and sour cream. Sift together soda, spices and flour, then add to creamed mixture. Chill the dough.

On a floured board, roll portions of dough into 1-inch (2.5 cm) rolls. Cut into ½-inch (1.2 cm) pieces. Place on greased cookie sheet. Bake at 350°F (180°C) for 10 minutes until nicely browned.

PECAN TASSIES

Cheese pastry:

1	3-ounce package cream cheese	85 g
½	cup butter	125 mL
1	cup flour	250 mL

Filling:

⅔	cup pecans, chopped	150 mL
1	egg	1
¾	cup brown sugar	175 mL
1	tablespoon margarine	15 mL
1	teaspoon vanilla	5 mL
	dash of salt	

Let cheese and butter soften at room temperature. Blend together. Stir in flour. Chill about 1 hour.

Shape into 2 dozen 1-inch balls. Place in ungreased 1¾-inch (4.5 cm) muffin pans. Press dough evenly against sides and bottoms of each one.

Beat together the egg, brown sugar, margarine, vanilla, and salt until smooth. Divide half of the pecans among the pastry lined pans. Add the egg mixture, and top with remaining pecans. Bake at 325°F (160°C) for 25 minutes, or until filling is set. Cool before removing from pans. Yield: 24

RASPBERRY BARS

Dough:

2	cups flour	500 mL
2	teaspoons baking powder	10 mL
½	cup margarine	125 mL
1	tablespoon milk	15 mL
1	egg, well beaten	1

Filling:

	Raspberry jam	
2	cups coconut	500 mL
2	tablespoons margarine	30 mL
1	teaspoon vanilla	5 mL
1½	cups sugar	375 mL
1	egg	1

Mix flour and baking powder. Cut in margarine until mixture resembles fine crumbs. Stir in milk and egg to make a soft dough. Line 8-inch (20 cm) square pan with dough. Cover with raspberry jam. Mix remaining ingredients and place over the jam layer. Bake at 350°F (180°C) for 45 minutes. Cut into bars while warm. Yield: 32 bars

BANANA TEA-SLICE

18	graham wafers	18
½	cup margarine	125 mL
½	cup icing sugar	125 mL
1	egg yolk	1
½	cup maraschino cherries, quartered	125 mL
½	cup walnuts, chopped	125 mL
½	cup banana, mashed	125 mL
1	teaspoon lemon juice	5 mL
1	cup coconut	250 mL
2	tablespoons butter	30 mL
1	cup icing sugar	250 mL
3	tablespoons maraschino cherry juice	45 mL

Line bottom of 8-inch (20 cm) square pan with graham wafers cut to fit correctly. Cream margarine, icing sugar and egg yolk together until fluffy. Stir in cherries, walnuts, bananas, lemon juice and coconut. Spread mixture evenly over wafers and cover with another layer of wafers. Press down lightly.

Cream butter and icing sugar, add cherry juice to make an icing of spreading consistency. Spread over cake.

Chill 24 hours. Cut into bars. Yield: 32 bars

MINT CREAM

This may be frozen.

1	envelope dessert topping	1
1	pint vanilla ice cream	500 mL
1½	ounces crème de menthe liqueur	30 mL

Make dessert topping as directed on package. Soften ice cream and add. Stir in crème de menthe to tint green. Serve in sherbet glasses. Garnish with green cherry. Yield: 6 servings

FROZEN BANANA-SPLIT DESSERT

This dessert will refreeze and keeps well.

2	cups graham-wafer crumbs	500 mL
¼	teaspoon salt	1 mL
1	tablespoon sugar	15 mL
½	cup butter or margarine	125 mL
3	bananas	3
½	gallon vanilla ice cream	2 L
	nuts (optional)	
1	cup chocolate chips	250 mL
½	cup butter	125 mL
2	cups icing sugar	500 mL
1½	cups evaporated milk	375 mL
1	teaspoon vanilla	5 mL
1	cup whipping cream	250 mL

Mix graham-wafer crumbs with salt and sugar; cut in butter. Pat into 9 x 13 inch (22 x 33 cm) pan reserving ½ cup (125 mL) for topping. Slice bananas over crust; spread on ice cream; sprinkle on nuts. Freeze.

Melt chocolate and butter. Add sugar, milk and cook until smooth and thick; add vanilla. Cool. Pour over ice cream and freeze. Whip the cream and spread over chocolate. Sprinkle on remaining crumbs.

Remove dessert from freezer a few minutes before serving. Yield: 24 servings

PEANUT BUTTER SLICE

⅓	cup margarine	75 mL
⅓	cup peanut butter	75 mL
½	cup brown sugar	125 mL
3	eggs	3
1	cup flour	250 mL
1	cup brown sugar	250 mL
1	teaspoon vanilla	5 mL
¼	cup flour	65 mL
½	teaspoon baking powder	2 mL
¾	cup coconut	175 mL
¾	cup cherries, chopped	175 mL

Cream margarine, peanut butter and ½ cup sugar (125 mL). Separate one egg and beat the yolk; add to the creamed mixture. Set aside the egg white. Mix in 1 cup (250 mL) flour. Place in 9-inch (22 cm) square pan; bake at 350°F (180°C) for 10 minutes.

Beat remaining eggs and egg white, add sugar, vanilla, flour, baking powder, coconut and cherries. Pour over baked crust. Bake at 350°F (180°C) for 25 to 30 minutes. Yield: 32 bars

CHERRY CREAM DESSERT

A delicious party dessert which may be made ahead and frozen.

1½	cups graham-wafer crumbs	375 mL
4	tablespoons icing sugar	60 mL
1	tablespoon flour	15 mL
½	cup melted butter	125 mL
1	19-ounce can cherry pie filling	540 mL
1	cup whipping cream	250 mL
2½	cups miniature marshmallows	625 mL

Combine crumbs, sugar, flour and butter. Press into 9-inch (22 cm) pan. Bake at 350°F (180°C) for 10 minutes. Remove from oven and cool.

Pour pie filling over crust. Whip cream, fold in marshmallows; spread over cherry filling. Chill overnight. Yield: 24 servings

CHOCOLATE DESSERT

2	cups graham wafer crumbs	500 mL
½	cup melted butter	125 mL
⅓	cup white sugar	75 mL
1	bar 2.79 ounces burnt almond chocolate	79 g
½	cup milk	125 mL
20	large marshmallows	20
½	pint whipping cream	250 mL

Butter an 8″ x 8″ (20 cm x 20 cm x 5 cm) pan. Combine graham wafers, sugar and melted butter. Save ¼ cup (60 mL) to spread on top, spread remainder in buttered pan. Melt chocolate bars, marshmallows, milk in top of double boiler over hot water. Cool and add ½ pint (250 mL) whipped cream. Spread on base. Sprinkle with remaining graham wafer mixture. Chill in refrigerator. May be frozen. Serves 10 to 12

EASTER BUNNY PIE

Pie shell:

2	tablespoons butter	30 mL
1½	cups flaked coconut	375 mL

Filling:

¾	cup milk	175 mL
1	ounce unsweetened chocolate	28 g
¼	teaspoon salt	1 mL
20	large marshmallows or 2½ cups miniature marshmallows	625 mL
1	teaspoon vanilla	5 mL
½	teaspoon peppermint flavoring	2 mL
1	cup whipping cream	250 mL

Melt butter, add coconut and combine thoroughly. Press into a 9-inch (22 cm) pie plate. Bake at 300°F (150°C) for 10 to 15 minutes.

Combine milk, chocolate, salt in top of double boiler. Cook over boiling water until chocolate is melted. Add marshmallows and stir until melted. Cool. Stir in vanilla and peppermint flavoring. Whip the cream until stiff; fold into cooled chocolate mixture. Pour into prepared pie shell. Chill until set.

To make marshmallow bunnies snip top of large marshmallow as if to cut a thin slice, but do not cut right through. Cut top slice almost in half to make ears. Stick toothpick halves through ears to hold them up. Make face using whole cloves for eyes and nose, and coconut for whiskers. Set bunnies on filling around the edge of the pie. Yield: 8 servings.

PINEAPPLE DREAM PIE

1	3-ounce package lemon jelly powder	85	g
1	3-ounce package vanilla-tapioca pudding	85	g
1¼	cups milk	315 mL	
1	14-ounce can crushed pineapple	398 mL	
1	cup whipping cream	250 mL	

Combine jelly powder and pudding mix and stir in milk. Cook stirring constantly until mixture thickens. Cool.

Add ⅓ cup (75 mL) of juice from pineapple. Whip the cream. Fold in pineapple and cream. Pour into pie shell (as prepared in Easter Bunny Pie, p. 89). Chill 5 to 6 hours. Yield: 8 servings

STRAWBERRY ICE-BOX CAKE

Good refrigerated overnight.

1	3-ounce package strawberry jelly powder	85	g
⅔	cup boiling water	165 mL	
5	large marshmallows	5	
1	15-ounce package frozen slice strawberries	425	g
2	envelopes dessert topping	2	
2	layers of white cake, cut in ½ to make 4 layers	2	

Dissolve jelly powder in boiling water. Add marshmallows and strawberries. Stir till smooth. When thoroughly cool, but not set, combine with 1 package of prepared dessert topping. Spread each layer.

Chill for 20 minutes in refrigerator, then stack layers together.

Complete dessert using second package of prepared topping and decorate with fresh strawberries before serving.

Strawberry Graham-Wafer Dessert:

2	cups graham-wafer crumbs	500 mL	
½	cup butter	125 mL	
½	cup brown sugar	125 mL	

Combine graham wafers, butter and brown sugar; reserve ½ cup (125 mL) for topping. Press remainder into 9-inch (20 cm) buttered square pan. Over this base spread filling from Strawberry Ice Box Cake (see recipe above). Sprinkle with reserved crumbs. Refrigerate. Yield: 12 servings

BUTTER TARTS

½	cup butter	125 mL
½	cup brown sugar	125 mL
1	cup syrup	250 mL
2	eggs, beaten	2
½	cup raisins	125 mL
½	cup walnuts, chopped	125 mL
¼	teaspoon nutmeg	2 mL
¼	teaspoon salt	2 mL

Soften butter, add brown sugar and syrup. Stir in eggs. Add raisins, walnuts, nutmeg and salt. Beat well. Spoon into unbaked tart shells. Bake at 400°F (200°C) for 10 to 15 minutes. Use low rack in oven. Yield: 24 tarts

ALMOND ICING OR PASTE

1	pound almonds	.5 kg
1	pound icing sugar	.5 kg
¼	teaspoon salt	1 mL
2	eggs, beaten	2
1	teaspoon rosewater	5 mL
½	teaspoon almond flavoring	2 mL
1	egg white, beaten	1

Blanch almonds, put through the food chopper or blender. Mix with icing sugar and salt. Mix in egg and flavoring to form a stiff paste.

Turn the mixture out on a board dusted with icing sugar and roll to desired size and shape. Brush cake with egg white, place on almond icing. With a rolling pin, lightly roll to a perfect smoothness. Let stand 24 hours before covering with white frosting.

POPCORN CHRISTMAS TREES

1⅓	cups icing sugar	325 mL
1	egg white	1
¼	teaspoon vinegar	1 mL
¼	cup popping corn	65 mL
	ice cream cones	

Mix icing sugar, egg white and vinegar for icing. Pop the corn. Turn cones upside down and cover with icing. Stick popcorn all over outside of cones. When dry, decorate with red cinnamon drops and silver dragees (attached with a spot of icing). Sprinkle with colored sugar.

AFTER DINNER MINTS

1	egg white	1
2	tablespoons water	30 mL
½	teaspoon essence of peppermint	2 mL
1	pound icing sugar coloring, if desired	.5 kg

Mix egg white, water, peppermint and coloring gently (4 or 5 strokes). Stir in icing sugar and knead as for bread dough. Take small pieces (size of an egg) and roll into shape of pencil. Cut with scissors and let drop on wax paper, not touching each other.

Leave for 24 hours. Then put on large plate until firm. Do not pack in closed container.

More sugar may be needed, especially if a large egg is used.

LOW CALORIE
LOW JOULE

LIFESTYLES have altered dramatically in a hundred years. For those who first settled along the Red River in Manitoba, the gruelling work schedule meant there was no need to count calories.

"Every article I wore was the product of my mother's hands, even my shoes, until I was fourteen or fifteen . . . we used to tan leather with willow bark in a tanning tub . . . when we worked in the fields there was always a great deal to be done in the evening. The milk had to be attended to and the skim milk fed to calves and the butter churned. We made a cheese usually on Saturday, using the rennet which we prepared from the stomach of calves. In the fall, after slaughtering, there was a great deal of work to be done in making blood puddings and white puddings and in boiling and drying tripe and getting our whole winter's supply of meat ready."

From Women of Red River, W. J. Healey
Bulman Bros. Ltd., Winnipeg, 1923.

Then within the century came the change to a sophisticated technological society. The advent of mechanization, a revolution of transportation and the proliferation of labor-saving devices of all kinds wrought a dramatic change in activity pattern. The colonist who in 1905 walked all day behind the plough and harrow eventually secured a harrow-cart with a seat so that he might ride. Horses were replaced by tractors. Great mechanical bale loaders took the heavy work out of getting in the hay. Physical work was lessened on the farm.

The homemaker who had once kept the family self-sufficient in food and clothing through her endless toil gave up the scrub board for a hand–turned washing machine. Later her daughter found relief in an automatic washer and dryer. Drudgery was gone but a new problem emerged. Abundance of food, labor-saving machines and the change from an active to a sedentary life style has resulted in concern about over-weight and obesity.

More people are living in towns and cities. For those who are office bound, regular meals are skipped and calorie-heavy snacks substituted. Whole families go out for special occasions to feast on chips, milkshakes and chocolate sundaes. Small wonder that fitness and exercise programs are promoted to maintain a balance of food intake and energy output.

Today nutrition, and particularly calorie consciousness, has become a preoccupation. Preparing meals that meet nutritional needs without supplying excess calories is a problem for the person who is older and whose physical activity has declined. So, too, for homemakers, anxious that their families develop good eating habits.

The low calorie recipes in this section make no pretense of being all-inclusive. They have been submitted by Saskatchewan W.I. members who have used them, acknowledging their own need for food that is both interesting, sparing of calories and generous in nutrients.

94

water along with chicken bouillon cubes and salt. Stir until all are dissolved; add lemon juice. Chill until partially set. Fold in pineapple and chicken. Turn into 1-quart (1 L) loaf pan. Unmold on crisp greens. Yield: 6 servings

REFRIGERATOR SALAD

Salad keeps well for 6 weeks.

3	pounds cabbage, shredded	1.5 kg
2	pounds carrots, shredded	1 kg
1	large onion, chopped	1
1	green pepper, chopped (optional)	1
¾	cup sugar	175 mL
1	cup oil	250 mL
2	teaspoons celery seed	10 mL
2	teaspoons salt	10 mL
1	cup vinegar	250 mL

Mix vegetables and sprinkle with ½ cup (125 mL) sugar. Heat (but do not boil) remainder of sugar, oil, celery seed, salt and vinegar; pour over vegetable mix. Pack in containers and store in refrigerator. Let stand 1 day before using.

VEGETABLE SALAD

1	3-ounce package lime jelly powder	85 g
¼	teaspoon salt	1 mL
1	cup boiling water	250 mL
½	cup cold water	125 mL
1½	tablespoons vinegar	25 mL
½	cup mayonnaise	125 mL
¾	cup cucumber, diced	175 mL
¾	cup celery, diced	175 mL
1	tablespoon onion, chopped	15 mL

Dissolve jelly powder and salt in boiling water. Add cold water, vinegar and mayonnaise. Beat to blend well. Fold in cucumber, celery, onion. Pour into a 1-quart (1 L) mold. Chill until firm. Yield: 6 servings

LETTUCE SALAD

Follow the recipe for Vegetable Salad, but substitute for the cucumber, celery and onion:

3	cups lettuce, coarsely chopped	750 mL
¼	cup green onion, sliced omit mayonnaise	65 mL

"I DON'T LIKE COTTAGE CHEESE" SALAD

1	3-ounce package lime jelly powder	85 g
1	cup hot water	250 mL
½	cup creamed cottage cheese	125 mL
1	14-ounce can pineapple chunks	398 mL
3	lettuce leaves	3
3	teaspoons mayonnaise	15 mL

Dissolve jelly in hot water. Add cottage cheese and pineapple, mix well. Chill in individual molds. Unmold on lettuce leaf and top with mayonnaise. Yield: 3 servings

SAVORY FRENCH DRESSING

1	cup vinegar	250 mL
¼	cup oil	65 mL
3	tablespoons brown sugar	45 mL
½	teaspoon paprika	2 mL
½	cup catsup	125 mL
3	tablespoons lemon juice	45 mL

Mix ingredients together; beat with electric mixer. Place in sealer with tight-fitting lid. Shake before using. Yield 2 cups (500 mL)

Tangy french dressing:
Follow the recipe for Savory French Dressing, then add:

1	cup cottage cheese	250 mL
1	tablespoon onion, grated	15 mL

FRENCH DRESSING

½	cup oil	125 mL
2	tablespoons vinegar or lemon juice	30 mL
2	teaspoons sugar	10 mL
¼	teaspoon salt	1 mL
¼	teaspoon paprika	1 mL
¼	teaspoon dry mustard	1 mL
1	clove garlic (optional)	1

Mix all ingredients in a sealer with a tight-fitting lid; shake well. Chill.

After 6 days remove garlic. Shake well before using. Yield: ½ cup (125 mL)

MAYONNAISE

Low calorie and made with a blender.

1	egg	1
2½	tablespoons vinegar	35 mL
½	teaspoon dry mustard	2 mL
1	tablespoon sugar	15 mL
¼	teaspoon salt	1 mL
2	teaspoons onion, minced	10 mL
1	cup cooking oil	250 mL

Put egg, vinegar, mustard, sugar, salt and onion in the blender; add ¼ cup (50 mL) of oil. Cover and blend at medium speed for 15 seconds. Remove cover and quickly add remainder of oil (all oil must be added in 15 seconds). Blend.

LOW CALORIE GREEN SALAD DRESSING

1	cup celery, chopped	250 mL
3	tablespoons onion flakes	45 mL
1	teaspoon sugar	5 mL
1	teaspoon vinegar	5 mL
1	large cucumber	1

Place celery, onion flakes, sugar and vinegar in electric blender. Cover and blend for 30 seconds until thick and smooth. Peel and chop cucumber and add to blender. Blend 30 seconds more. Store in covered container in refrigerator. Yield: 1½ cups (375 mL)

THOUSAND ISLAND DRESSING

2	tablespoons mayonnaise	30 mL
2	tablespoons chili sauce	30 mL
1	teaspoon onion flakes	5 mL
1	teaspoon dill pickle, minced	5 mL
½	teaspoon parsley, minced	2 mL

Combine ingredients. Refrigerate for 15 minutes before serving. Yield: 2 servings

SALAD DRESSING

½	teaspoon mustard	2 mL
½	teaspoon salt	2 mL
1	tablespoon flour	15 mL
1	tablespoon sugar	15 mL
½	teaspoon celery seed	2 mL
¼	cup skim milk	65 mL
1	egg, beaten	1
3	tablespoons vinegar	45 mL

Combine mustard, salt, flour, sugar and celery seed in top of double boiler. Add milk slowly, stirring until thickened. Cover and cook for 8 minutes. Add beaten egg, cook 3 minutes, stirring constantly. Remove from heat; stir in vinegar. Store in refrigerator.

LOW CALORIE SALAD DRESSING

2	tablespoons cornstarch	30 mL
½	teaspoon salt	2 mL
½	teaspoon dry mustard	2 mL
¼	teaspoon celery seed (optional)	1 mL
1½	cups water	375 mL
⅓	cup vinegar	75 mL
3	tablespoons sugar	45 mL
2	eggs	2

Combine cornstarch, salt, mustard, and celery seed in top of double boiler. Combine water, vinegar, and sugar. Add small amount of liquid mixture to dry mixture making a paste. Add remainder of liquid, stirring until smooth. Beat eggs and add to mixture. Cook over boiling water until thick. Cool with lid on. Yield: 2 cups (500 mL)

ZERO SALAD DRESSING

½	cup tomato juice	125 mL
2	tablespoons lemon juice	30 mL
1	tablespoon onion, grated	15 mL
¼	teaspoon salt	1 mL
⅛	teaspoon pepper	.5 mL

Put all ingredients in the blender; blend 10 seconds. Place in a sealer with tight-fitting lid. Shake well before using. Yield: 1 cup (250 mL)

Spicy salad dressing:
Follow the recipe for Zero Salad Dressing, then add:

1	teaspoon parsley	5 mL
1	teaspoon green pepper, chopped	5 mL
1	teaspoon mustard	5 mL
1	teaspoon horseradish	5 mL

Smooth salad dressing:
Follow the recipe for Zero Salad Dressing, then add:

2	tablespoons cooking oil	30 mL

ZESTY SALAD DRESSING

½	teaspoon gelatine	2 mL
1	tablespoon cold water	15 mL
¼	cup boiling water	50 mL
1	tablespoon sugar	15 mL
½	teaspoon salt	2 mL
1	teaspoon lemon rind, grated	5 mL
½	cup lemon juice	125 mL
⅛	teaspoon dry mustard	.5 mL
⅛	teaspoon black pepper	.5 mL
¼	teaspoon paprika	1 mL
¼	teaspoon onion juice	1 mL
2	tablespoons parsley	30 mL
	few grains cayenne	

Soak gelatine in cold water for 5 minutes. Add boiling water and stir until dissolved; add sugar and salt. Cool. Add remaining ingredients. Store in sealer with tight-fitting lid. Chill. Shake well before serving. Yield: ¾ cup (175 mL)

LOW CALORIE SOUP

1	48-ounce can tomato juice	1.36 L
1	tablespoon lemon juice	15 mL
3	tablespoons onion flakes	45 mL
3	beef bouillon cubes	3
½	cup water	125 mL
3	cups cabbage, shredded	750 mL

Bring tomato juice, lemon juice and onion flakes to a boil. Add beef bouillon, water and cabbage. Simmer 15 minutes. Serve hot.

Slim soup:
Follow the recipe for Low Calorie Soup, then add:

1	cup celery, chopped	250 mL
1	cup green beans	250 mL
½	cup mushrooms	125 mL

MARY'S DUTCH-STYLE SPLIT PEA SOUP

5	ounces green split peas	150 g
2	cups celery, diced	500 mL
4	ounces leeks, chopped	100 g
2	chicken bouillon cubes	2
3	ounces cooked ham	90 g
1	teaspoon salt	5 mL
¼	teaspoon pepper	1 mL

Soak peas overnight in cold clean water (water should cover the peas).

Next day add celery, leeks and chicken bouillon cubes. Simmer 1½ hours with pot tightly covered. When cooked, add ham, salt and pepper.

DEVILLED CHICKEN BONES

2	chicken drumsticks	2
2	chicken thighs	2
1	teaspoon salt	5 mL
½	teaspoon pepper	2 mL
1	cup tomato sauce	250 mL
2	tablespoons Worcestershire sauce	30 mL
2	teaspoons prepared mustard	10 mL
1	teaspoon imitation butter flavoring	5 mL

Skin chicken. Sprinkle chicken with salt and pepper and brown lightly in a non-stick skillet. Cut 4 small gashes in chicken before putting into baking dish. Combine remaining ingredients; and pour over the chicken. Bake at 350°F (180°C) for 25 minutes. Yield: 2 servings

CHICKEN TERIYAKI

1	frying chicken	1.5 kg
½	cup soya sauce	125 mL
⅓	cup rice wine vinegar	75 mL
1	teaspoon garlic powder	5 mL
3	tablespoons sugar	45 mL
1½	teaspoons ginger	7 mL

Cut chicken in serving-sized portions; remove skin. Make marinade by mixing remaining ingredients. Place chicken in shallow baking dish and pour on marinade.

Cover and let stand in refrigerator for one hour. Bake at 325°F (160°C) until chicken is tender. Baste with marinade several times while cooking. Yield: 4 servings

NOTE: It is preferable to use Japanese soya sauce and rice wine vinegar.

BAKED CHICKEN AND RICE CASSEROLE

1	cup rice, uncooked	250 mL
2	10-ounce cans mushroom stems and pieces	568 mL
1	frying chicken	1.5 kg
2	cups onion, sliced	500 mL
2	cups skim milk	500 mL
2	tablespoons flour	30 mL
1	teaspoon salt	5 mL
¼	teaspoon pepper	1 mL

Place rice in 2-quart (2 L) casserole. Drain mushrooms; save liquid and pour over rice. Soak for 1 hour.

Cut chicken into serving-sized pieces. Place chicken on rice, cover with a layer of onions, then a layer of mushrooms. Combine milk with flour, salt and pepper. Pour over rice. Bake, covered, at 350°F (180°C) for 1 hour; uncover and continue to bake 1 hour longer. Yield: 6 servings

CHICKEN CACCIATORE

1	chicken breast	1
3	cups tomato juice	750 mL
3	tablespoons onion, diced	45 mL
1	bay leaf	1
1	tablespoon Italian dressing	15 mL
1	tablespoon parsley	15 mL
½	teaspoon oregano	2 mL
1	cup green pepper, chopped	250 mL
½	cup peas	125 mL
1	10-ounce can mushrooms	284 mL

Remove skin from chicken breast. Place in skillet and add tomato juice, onion, bay leaf, Italian dressing, parsley and oregano. Simmer 1 hour.

Add peppers, peas and mushrooms and cook for another 15 minutes. Serve with spaghetti. Yield: 2 servings

PORK CHINESE-STYLE

This is a very versatile recipe — other low calorie vegetables can be added.

4	ounces cooked pork-butt steak	125 g
1	cup green pepper	250 mL
1	cup celery, diced	250 mL
¼	cup onion, diced	65 mL
1	teaspoon salt	5 mL
¼	teaspoon pepper	1 mL
1	cup mushrooms, cooked	250 mL
1	teaspoon soya sauce	5 mL
1	teaspoon ginger	5 mL
1	beef bouillon cube	1
¾	cup water	175 mL
¼	teaspoon agar (optional)	1 mL

Cut pork into bite-sized pieces. Mix with remainder of ingredients except agar; heat over medium heat until hot enough to serve. If desired, the mixture may be thickened by adding the agar dissolved in a little water. Yield: 4 servings

OXTAILS WITH HERBS

3	pounds oxtails	1.5 kg
2	tablespoons fat	30 mL
½	cup onion, sliced	125 mL
2	teaspoons salt	10 mL
¼	teaspoon pepper	1 mL
½	teaspoon thyme	2 mL
½	cup tomato juice	125 mL

Cut meat into 2-inch (5 cm) serving-sized pieces. Brown in fat; add onion and cook slightly, then add seasonings and tomato juice.

Cook 30 minutes in pressure-saucepan at 15 pounds pressure (103.35 kPa). Allow pressure-saucepan to cool slowly.

If preferred, cook in oven at 325°F (160°C) for 3 hours. Tomato juice should be increased to 3 cups (750 mL). Yield 6 servings

PINEAPPLE MEAT LOAF

3	pineapple slices	3
1	pound lean ground beef	.5 kg
1	cup ground veal	250 mL
1	cup soft bread crumbs	250 mL
¾	cup skim milk	175 mL
½	cup onion, chopped	125 mL
1	egg, beaten	1
1	teaspoon salt	5 mL
¼	teaspoon paprika	1 mL
¼	teaspoon marjoram	1 mL
¼	teaspoon thyme	1 mL
¼	teaspoon pepper	1 mL

Grease 9 x 5 inch (22 x 12 cm) loaf pan. Cut 2 pineapple slices in halves and arrange in an attractive pattern in the bottom of the pan. Mix together all the other ingredients. Pack lightly in pan. Bake at 350°F (180°C) for 1 hour. Invert on a platter for serving. Yield: 6 servings

VEGETABLE MEAT LOAF

A glossy brown appetizing loaf with a surprise center.

½	cup carrot, sliced	125 mL
½	cup onion, chopped	125 mL
½	cup green pepper, chopped	125 mL
¼	cup celery, sliced	50 mL
1	tomato	1
2	slices bread, chunks	2
1	egg	1
1	teaspoon salt	5 mL
½	teaspoon Worcestershire sauce	2 mL
1	pound lean ground beef	.5 kg

Chop carrot, onion, green pepper and celery coarsely in a blender. Empty into a saucepan and add tomato (peeled and cut). Cover and simmer for eight minutes.

Put bread, egg, salt and Worcestershire sauce in blender. Blend smooth. Empty into bowl and add ground beef. Mix well. Turn meat mixture out onto baking surface and pat into a rectangle 8 x 10 inches (25 x 30 cm). Spread vegetable mixture over center of meat. Roll meat around vegetables; seal seams and ends. Place roll in baking dish. Bake at 350°F (180°C) for 50 minutes. Yield 5 servings

SWEET AND SOUR VEAL

1½	pounds ground veal, bite size	.75 kg
1½	cups tomato juice	375 mL
1	14-ounce can bean sprouts	398 mL
½	cup onion, chopped	125 mL
2	cups celery, chopped	500 mL
½	cup green pepper, chopped	125 mL
6	slices unsweetened pineapple	6
½	cup unsweetened pineapple juice	125 mL
4	tablespoons vinegar	60 mL
2	tablespoons soya sauce	30 mL
4	tablespoons sugar	60 mL

Brown veal in frying pan, stirring often. Drain off excess fat. Add remaining ingredients and simmer slowly over low heat for 20 minutes. Yield: 8 servings

BRAISED STEAK

1	pound round steak	.5 kg
1	cup onions, chopped	250 mL
½	cup green pepper, chopped	125 mL
1	cup tomatoes, chopped	250 mL
½	cup beef bouillon	125 mL
½	teaspoon salt	2 mL

Trim fat from meat, cut into serving-sized pieces and place in shallow baking dish. Add vegetables and beef bouillon; season with salt. Cook at 350°F (180°C) for 1 hour until meat is tender. Yield: 4 servings

OVEN-BAKED STEAK

2	pounds round steak	1 kg
2	tablespoons cooking oil	30 mL
½	cup onion, chopped	125 mL
1	10-ounce can mushroom stems and pieces	284 mL
1	tablespoon Worcestershire sauce	15 mL
1	teaspoon salt	5 mL
¼	teaspoon pepper	1 mL
¼	teaspoon garlic salt (optional)	1 mL
3	tablespoons flour (optional)	45 mL

Cut steak in serving-sized pieces. Brown in oil in heavy pan; pour off oil. Add onions, mushrooms (including liquid). Reduce heat; add seasonings and water to cover. To thicken, mix flour with water and add to mixture. Bake at 350°F (180°C) for 1½ hours or until steak is tender. Yield: 6 servings

NO-GAIN VEGETABLE MARROW CASSEROLE

Vegetable marrow is one variety of Summer Squash.

1½	pound vegetable marrow	750 mL
½	cup onion sliced	125 mL
1	cup corn flakes, crushed	250 mL
1	teaspoon diet margarine	5 mL

Wash and pare marrow; cut in cubes. Place layer of marrow in greased 1½-quart (1.5 L) casserole. Cover with layer of onion and layer of corn flakes. Repeat layers until casserole is nearly full ending with cornflake layer. Bake at 350°F (180°C) for about 45 minutes. Yield: 6 servings

SALMON MUFFIN

1	7¾-ounce can salmon	220 g
¼	cup onion, minced	50 mL
2	teaspoons green relish	10 mL
4	teaspoons salad dressing	20 mL
2	eggs, beaten	2

Drain, remove skin and bones and flake salmon; add remaining ingredients and toss together lightly. Half-fill well-greased individual baking dishes. Place in pan of hot water and bake at 350°F (180°C) for 30 minutes. Yield: 4 servings

SALMON LOAF

2	7¾-ounce cans salmon	440 g
1	cup fine bread crumbs	250 mL
½	cup onion, chopped	125 mL
2	eggs, beaten	2
1	tablespoon lemon juice	15 mL
1	10-ounce can cream of celery soup	284 mL
½	cup milk	125 mL

Drain the salmon, saving liquid. Remove skin and bones from salmon, flake salmon and mix with bread crumbs, onion, egg and lemon juice. Pack into well-greased 9 x 5 inch (22 x 12 cm) loaf pan. Bake at 375°F (190°C) for 1 hour until nicely browned. Cool in pan for 10 minutes. Then loosen from sides of pan and turn loaf out on platter.

To make celery sauce, mix celery soup with milk and simmer for a few minutes. Serve sauce in a dish with salmon loaf. Yield: 6 servings

SHRIMP AND MUSHROOMS

2	tablespoons butter	30 mL
2	cups celery, chopped	500 mL
1	10-ounce can mushrooms	284 mL
1	tablespoon soya sauce	15 mL
1	teaspoon ginger	5 mL
1	tablespoon cornstarch	15 mL
1	tablespoon water	15 mL
½	cup beef broth	125 mL
2	4½-ounce cans shrimp	226 mL
2	cups cooked rice	500 mL

In large frying pan melt butter. Add celery, mushrooms, soya sauce, ginger and pepper. Cook and stir until celery is tender. Mix cornstarch, water and broth and add to vegetable mixture. Cook until mixture thickens. Add shrimp, heat thoroughly.

Serve over hot rice. Yield: 4 servings

SKINNY BAKE

Add your favorite seasonings.

4	cups very fine dry bread crumbs	1 L
½	cup cooking oil	125 mL
1	tablespoon salt	15 mL
1	tablespoon paprika	15 mL
1	tablespoon celery seed	15 mL
1	teaspoon pepper	5 mL

Empty bread crumbs into a bowl. Over these sprinkle oil, toss with a fork until crumbs are well coated. Add seasonings; mix thoroughly. Store in refrigerator until ready to use.

Place a small quantity in a plastic bag along with pieces of chicken, meat or fish; shake until well coated.

HOW TO SPROUT SOYBEANS

Sort beans, discarding split or shriveled beans; wash beans. Cover beans with lukewarm water, allowing 4 cups (1 L) of water for each cup (250 mL) of beans. Soak overnight.

Drain beans in a colander, rinse with fresh water. Place the soaked beans in a glass sealer (2-quart (2 L) jar is about right for 1 cup (250 mL) of beans). Cover mouth of sealer with cheesecloth, fasten in place with elastic band. Invert jar so water can drain away.

Three or four times each day, remove the cloth, fill the jar with lukewarm water and flush the beans off. Drain and return to dark warm storage.

Beans will be ready for use in 3 to 5 days. Sprouted beans should be kept refrigerated like any fresh vegetable.

ZUCCHINI BREAD STUFFING

3	cups bread cubes	750 mL
½	cup celery, diced	125 mL
½	cup onion, chopped	125 mL
2	tablespoons margarine	30 mL
4	cups zucchini, chopped	1 L
1	egg, beaten	1
2	tablespoons parsley	30 mL
1½	teaspoons salt	7 mL
1	teaspoon poultry dressing	5 mL
¼	teaspoon pepper	1 mL

Toast bread cubes in oven at 350°F (180°C) for 20 minutes. Cook celery and onion in margarine for 20 minutes. Add bread cubes, zucchini, egg, parsley, salt, poultry dressing and pepper. Mix well. Yield: stuffing for approximately 6-pound (3 kg) chicken

ZUCCHINI CASSEROLE

6	cups zucchini squash, thinly sliced	1.5 L
1	cup boiling water	250 mL
4	teaspoons butter	20 mL
4	teaspoons flour	20 mL
1	teaspoon salt	5 mL
½	cup milk	125 mL
2	eggs	2
½	teaspoon Worcestershire sauce	2 mL
1	teaspoon onion, minced	5 mL
¼	cup fine bread crumbs	65 mL
1	tablespoon butter, melted	15 mL

Prepare zucchini, cook in boiling water for 5 minutes; drain. Melt butter, blend in flour and salt; gradually add milk. Stir and cook until thick. Beat eggs, stir a little sauce into eggs, then gradually stir egg mixture into sauce. Add Worcestershire sauce, onion and zucchini. Place in 1½-quart (1.5 L) greased casserole. Mix bread crumbs and butter, sprinkle over casserole. Bake at 325°F (160°C) for 35 minutes. Yield: 6 servings

ZUCCHINI AU GRATIN

3	cups zucchini squash	750 mL
⅓	cup onion, diced	85 mL
1	teaspoon butter	5 mL
1	tablespoon water	15 mL
¼	cup Parmesan cheese, grated	65 mL
½	teaspoon salt	2 mL
¼	teaspoon pepper	1 mL

Cut zucchini in ½-inch (1.2 cm) slices. Sauté onion in butter; add zucchini and water. Cover and simmer until tender. Stir in cheese; season with salt and pepper. Yield: 4 servings

MARINATED CUCUMBERS

1	small onion	1
1	medium cucumber	1
½	cup vinegar	125 mL
½	cup water	125 mL
2	tablespoons sugar	30 mL
½	teaspoon salt	2 mL

Slice cucumber and onion. Mix vinegar, water, sugar and salt; pour over cucumber and onion. Cover and refrigerate 2 hours. Drain and serve. Yield: 4 to 6 servings

CREAMED DICED TURNIPS

4	cups turnips, cubed	1 L
4	tablespoons butter	60 mL
4	tablespoons flour	60 mL
½	teaspoon salt	2 mL
¼	teaspoon pepper	1 mL
¼	teaspoon nutmeg	1 mL
2	teaspoons sugar	10 mL
2	cups hot skim milk	500 mL

Cook turnips in salted boiling water until tender; drain. Melt butter, blend in flour, salt, pepper, nutmeg and sugar; gradually add milk. Stir and cook until sauce is thick. Add turnip and mix carefully. Yield: 8 servings

SAUERKRAUT IN WHITE WINE

This sauerkraut is particularly good when served with pork, roast duck, roast goose or grilled pork chops.

¼	cup onion, minced	65 mL
2	tablespoons butter	30 mL
1	quart sauerkraut, drained	1 L
1	cup tart apple, diced	250 mL
1	teaspoon caraway seed	5 mL
1	cup chicken bouillon	250 mL
1	cup dry white wine	250 mL

Sauté onion in butter. Add sauerkraut with apple and caraway seed. Turn into greased 1½-quart (1.5 L) casserole. Add chicken stock and white wine. Bake, covered, at 350°F (180°C) for 45 minutes to 1½ hours. Use shorter time for canned sauerkraut and longer time for bulk sauerkraut. Yield: 6 servings

NOTE: If sauerkraut is salty, rinse with cold water before cooking.

CEREAL PUFFS

3	egg whites	3
¾	cup sugar	175 mL
4	cups Special K cereal	1 L

In large bowl of electric mixer, beat egg whites until foamy. Beat in sugar, one tablespoon at a time. Continue beating until very stiff and glossy. Fold in cereal. Drop by spoonfuls on lightly greased cookie sheets. Bake at 300°F (150°C) for about 20 minutes or until lightly browned. Yield: 48 cookies

CHOCOLATE MOUSSE

1	envelope gelatine	1
¼	cup water	50 mL
3	tablespoons cocoa	45 mL
1	tablespoon cooking oil	15 mL
¼	cup icing sugar	50 mL
⅔	cup sugar	150 mL
¾	cup skim milk	175 mL
1	teaspoon vanilla	5 mL
½	teaspoon almond extract	2 mL
⅔	cup skim-milk powder	165 mL
½	cup ice water	125 mL
1	teaspoon lemon juice	5 mL

Soak gelatine in water for 5 minutes. Combine cocoa, cooking oil, sugars and milk in saucepan. Stir over medium heat until dissolved; add flavorings. Chill over cold water until mixture thickens. Combine skim milk powder, water and lemon juice and beat until mixture stands in firm peaks. Fold into chocolate mixture. Pour into molds or a baked pie shell. Yield: 6 servings

CHEESECAKE

2	envelopes gelatine	14 g
½	cup skim milk	125 mL
1	cup scalded milk	250 mL
2	teaspoons lemon rind, grated	10 mL
1	tablespoon lemon juice	15 mL
1	cup sugar	250 mL
2	eggs, separated	2
¼	teaspoon salt	1 mL
3	cups dry cottage cheese	750 mL
1	teaspoon vanilla	5 mL
⅔	cup graham wafer crumbs	150 mL

Sprinkle gelatine over cold milk; allow to dissolve for 5 minutes. Add scalded milk; mix until gelatine is thoroughly dissolved. Stir in lemon rind, lemon juice, ¾ cup (175 mL) sugar, egg yolks and salt.

Beat cottage cheese on high speed of mixer for 3 minutes. Stir into gelatine mixture. Add vanilla and chill until partially set.

Beat egg whites very stiff, adding remaining sugar. Fold gelatine mixture into the egg whites. Place one half of the graham-wafer crumbs into an 8-inch (20 cm) square pan. Cover with filling and sprinkle with remainder of the wafer crumbs. Chill until firm. Yield: 12 servings

HAWAIIAN DELIGHT CHEESECAKE

Follow recipe for Cheesecake with addition of a garnish of

1	14-ounce can pineapple tidbits drained	398 mL

COFFEE DELIGHT

2	tablespoons sugar	30 mL
½	envelope gelatine	½
1	tablespoon instant coffee	15 mL
1	cup skim milk	250 mL
1	egg yolk, beaten	1
1	egg white	1
½	teaspoon vanilla	2 mL

In top of double boiler combine sugar, gelatine, coffee and salt. In small bowl mix egg yolk and ½ cup (125 mL) of the milk. Add milk mixture to dry ingredients in double boiler. Cook, stirring frequently until gelatine dissolves. Remove from heat, add remainder of milk.

Chill until partially set. Add egg white and vanilla. Beat until mixture stands in firm peaks. Spoon into serving dishes and chill until firm. Yield: 6 servings

PINEAPPLE ORANGE CRÈME

This dessert can be frozen

1	cup graham-wafer crumbs	250 mL
1	tablespoon diet margarine	15 mL
½	cup skim milk powder	125 mL
½	cup orange juice, chilled	125 mL
1	egg white	1
1	tablespoon lemon juice	15 mL
¼	cup sugar	50 mL
1	14-ounce can crushed pineapple, drained	398 mL

Combine crumbs and margarine; reserve ¼ cup (50 mL) for topping. Sprinkle rest of mixture into 8-inch (20 cm) square pan.

Measure into mixing bowl skim milk powder, orange juice and egg white. Beat at high speed for 3 minutes. Add lemon juice. Continue beating 3 minutes longer. Turn mixer to low speed and add sugar. Fold in well–drained pineapple. Pour mixture over crumbs in pan. Top with reserve-crumbs.

Chill overnight. Yield: 9 servings

FRUIT SUPREME

2	envelopes gelatine	14 g
½	cup hot water	125 mL
½	cup fruit	125 mL
1	cup diet soda	250 mL
⅓	cup skim milk powder	75 mL
2	ice cubes	2

Blend boiling water and gelatine in blender (set on high speed) for 20 seconds. Add remaining ingredients and blend until thick. Pour into individual serving dishes. Yield: 6 servings

LIME SNOW

A light refreshing dessert.

1	3-ounce package lime jelly powder	85 g
2	cups boiling water	500 mL
1	egg white	1

Dissolve jelly powder in boiling water. Chill until set, but not firm. Whip until light and fluffy. Beat egg white until stiff. Fold in gelatine mixture. Yield: 5 servings

LEMON SNOW

1	envelope gelatine	1
¼	cup cold water	50 mL
1	cup boiling water	250 mL
½	cup white sugar	125 mL
¼	teaspoon lemon rind, grated	1 mL
⅓	cup lemon juice	75 mL

Soak gelatine in cold water for 5 minutes, then dissolve in boiling water. Add sugar, lemon rind and lemon juice; stir well. Chill over cold water until mixture thickens. Beat until foamy, then fold in whipped topping or Whipped Cream Substitute (see recipes p. 115). Turn into mold and chill until firm.

WHIPPED TOPPING

½	cup cold water	125 mL
1	tablespoon lemon juice	15 mL
⅔	cup skim milk powder	150 mL
¼	teaspoon salt	1 mL
¼	cup sugar	50 mL

Chill small bowl from food mixer. Combine water and lemon juice; add skim milk powder and salt. Beat until mixture stands in firm peaks; gradually add sugar. Serve immediately. Yield: 4 cups (1 L)

WHIPPED CREAM SUBSTITUTE

This mixture can be frozen and beaten again later if it loses its texture.

½	cup skim milk powder	125 mL
½	cup ice water	125 mL
1	egg white	1
1	tablespoon lemon juice	15 mL
½	teaspoon vanilla	2 mL
¼	cup sugar	50 mL

Chill small bowl from food mixer. Combine skim milk powder, water and egg white and place in bowl. Beat at high speed until egg whites are fluffy. Add lemon juice and beat for 1 minute more. Gradually add vanilla and sugar, beat until very fluffy. Serve immediately. Yield: 4 cups

CUSTARD SAUCE

2	eggs	2
¼	teaspoon salt	1 mL
¼	cup sugar	50 mL
1	cup skim milk powder	250 mL
¾	cup cold water	175 mL
1	cup hot water	250 mL
½	teaspoon vanilla	2 mL

Beat eggs; add salt, sugar, skim milk powder and cold water. Gradually stir in hot water. Cook, stirring constantly over hot (not boiling) water until mixture coats a spoon. Remove from heat; cool. Stir in vanilla. Yield: 2 cups (500 mL)

LOW-CAL JAM

4	tablespoons orange juice	60 mL
1	envelope unflavored gelatine	1
2	cups strawberries	500 mL

Dissolve gelatine in orange juice. Stir in strawberries. Boil for 3 minutes. Cool, then refrigerate.

NEVER-FAIL YOGURT

1	pound can evaporated milk	454 g
2	cups warm water	500 mL
½	cup sugar	125 mL
¾	cup skim milk powder	175 mL
¾	cup commercial yogurt	175 mL

Blend canned milk, warm water, sugar, and milk powder in blender for 10 seconds. Add commercial yogurt. Blend another 10 seconds.

Pour mixture into yogurt-maker and process 3 to 4 hours, or put jar of yogurt in a water bath in an oven at 115°F (45°C) for 7 to 8 hours until it reaches a thick consistency.

Refrigerate yogurt immediately. Honey, syrup, or molasses may be used in place of sugar.

SIMPLE HOMEMADE YOGURT

Many kinds of milk may be used for this recipe: whole, skim diluted, evaporated or reconstituted powder.

4	cups milk	1 L
3	tablespoons commercial yogurt	45 mL

Heat the milk to lukewarm, then mix in yogurt. This is blended easily if first mixed with ½ cup (125 mL) of milk. Divide into custard cups or pour into wide-mouthed jar and set in warm place, near a radiator or in a bowl of hot water. Keep the yogurt warm without cooking it.

Let stand for 6 to 8 hours or overnight (until it looks like a soft jelly). Then refrigerate 12 to 24 hours before using.

WHOLE GRAIN

WHEAT AND western Canada! One cannot think about one without thinking of the other. The impact of wheat upon the growth and fortune of the Canadian nation is incalculable.

But the prairie was not easily won over to wheat. Drought, grasshoppers, migrations of birds, invasions of mice, and flood afflicted planting in the first ten years.

Changes came through further calamity. In 1875 a grasshopper plague wiped out the total crop. Red Fife, the new variety purchased in the United States, grew well in Manitoba. Indeed, it grew so well that the 260 bushels planted yielded enough for a sale of wheat to Ontario in 1876. The export trade in wheat, destined to become of major importance to the western Canadian economy, had begun.

It would be agreeable to say that Canadian prairie dwellers, growing the best wheat in the world, prized the whole grain berry for their daily bread, but this was hardly the truth.

The Selkirk settlers, exporting their first shipment of wheat, soon felt the impact of consumer demand. Hungarian rolling mills which crushed the whole kernel, making separation of bran and germ from the flour easy, were installed by Ogilvies in Winnipeg in 1881. Through them white flour had become a reality.

Ethnic groups of settlers in Alberta and Saskatchewan were happy with their familiar dark bread, but were soon made to feel that is was not the fashion. The notion, transplanted from Europe, that white flour now had prestige, affected attitudes on the Canadian prairie. Today people worry that in spite of fortification, nutrients of vital importance are still missing from white bread. The solution for some has been to turn to whole grain products in which the bran, germ and endosperm of the grain are retained.

Homemakers who cannot immediately renounce the open texture of white bread are advised to use at least some all purpose flour in whole grain recipes. The bread will rise better and the family may be gradually won over to the whole grain philosophy.

A final piece of advice should be passed along to converts to whole grain cookery. If a range in the quantity of flour is given, always start with the minimum. Flours vary in moisture content according to the weather, the altitude, the length and place of storage. Stirring in too much flour is a mistake with any bread, and this is particularly true in the case of whole grain bread. It needs all the encouragement it can get.

Members of Women's Institutes, ever conscious about nutrition of the family, were quick to realize the importance of re-introducing the family to the use of whole grains.

It is a matter of re-education. Whole grain products are different from those baked with all purpose flour, different in taste and texture, different in color, with visible specks of bran and germ. Whole grain flours are low in gluten resulting in a bread that is moist, dense, and chewy. Some of the recipes in this section for whole grain bread will be compact, but ever so nourishing.

HARVEST GRANOLA BREAD

1	cup warm water	250 mL
1	package yeast	8 g
½	teaspoon salt	2 mL
1	tablespoon honey or molasses	15 mL
2	tablespoons oil	30 mL
2-2½	cups flour	500-625 mL
1¼	cups granola	300 mL

Dissolve yeast in water; let stand 10 minutes. Stir in salt, honey or molasses, oil and half of the flour; beat well. Add granola, stir in remainder of flour to make a stiff dough. Turn out on lightly-floured surface and knead. Cover; let rise until double in bulk.

Punch down and shape into a loaf. Place in greased 9 x 5 inch (20 x 12 cm) pan.

Cover and let rise. Bake at 350°F (180°C) for 45 minutes. Serve hot. Yield: 1 large loaf

WHOLE WHEAT FRENCH BREAD

2	tablespoons sugar	30 mL
3¼	cups warm water	800 mL
2	packages yeast	16 g
1	tablespoon salt	15 mL
2½	cups whole wheat flour	625 mL
4½	cups flour	1125 mL
	cornmeal	
1	egg white	1
1	tablespoon cold water	15 mL

Dissolve sugar in water; sprinkle on yeast. Let stand 10 minutes, then stir well. Add salt and whole wheat flour, mixing well. Beat in remaining flour to make a soft dough. Turn out onto lightly floured surface. Knead until smooth and elastic. Place in greased bowl, let rise until double in bulk.

Punch dough down; turn out on lightly floured board. Divide in half. Cover and let rest 10 minutes. Roll each half into a 15x10 inch (40x25 cm) rectangle. Beginning at wide side, roll up tightly like a jelly roll; seal edges well. Taper ends by rolling gently back and forth. Place loaves on greased baking sheets sprinkled with cornmeal.

Cover; let rise until double in bulk, about 1 hour. With sharp knife make several diagonal cuts on top of each loaf. Brush with slightly beaten egg white, then sprinkle with sesame seeds. Bake at 400°F (200°C) for 25 minutes. Quickly brush the loaves with cold water, return to oven for 10 minutes. Remove from baking sheets and cool on wire racks. Yield: 2 loaves

OVER-NIGHT BUNS

1	teaspoon sugar	5 mL
½	cup warm water	125 mL
1	package yeast	8 g
4	cups hot water	1 L
¾	cup lard	175 mL
2	teaspoons salt	10 mL
¾	cup white sugar	175 mL
10-12	cups flour	2.5-3 L

Dissolve sugar in water; sprinkle in yeast. Let stand 10 minutes. Stir lard into hot water, let cool. Stir in salt, sugar, then yeast mixture. Place flour in large bowl, gradually add the liquid, stirring carefully with a spoon until you have to use your hands. Cover and let rise.

Two hours later knead down. Two hours later put in pans.

In the morning, bake at 400°F (200°C) for 10 minutes. Yield: 60 to 80 buns.

Follow the schedule below when preparing overnight buns.
Mix at 5:00 p.m.
Knead down at 7:00 p.m.
Put in pans at 9:00 p.m.

ROYAL HIBERNIAN IRISH BROWN BREAD

5	cups whole-wheat flour	1.25 L
2½	cups all purpose flour	625 mL
⅓	cup sugar	75 mL
1	teaspoon salt	5 mL
2	teaspoons baking soda	10 mL
1	cup butter or margarine	250 mL
2	eggs	2
2¾	cups buttermilk or sour milk	675 mL

In a large bowl, mix together flours, sugar, salt and baking soda. Work in butter until mixture resembles fine crumbs. Beat eggs until foamy; then stir in sour milk. Make a well in the center of the dry ingredients and add egg mixture. Mix by hand until a stiff dough is formed. Turn onto a floured baking surface and knead well. Divide dough into 2 round balls. Flatten tops slightly and with a sharp knife cut an X in the top of each. Place loaves on baking sheet. Bake at 375°F (190°C) for 1 hour. Yield: 2 loaves

WHOLE WHEAT MUFFINS

1 ½	cups whole wheat flour (home-ground flour if available)	375 mL
½	cup flour	125 mL
1	tablespoon baking powder	15 mL
3	tablespoons sugar	45 mL
1	teaspoon salt	5 mL
1	egg	1
1 ½	cups milk	375 mL
¼	cup cooking oil	65 mL

Mix dry ingredients. Stir in liquids until just blended. Fill muffin cups ⅔ full. Bake at 400°F (200°C) for 15 minutes. Yield: 12 muffins

PUMPKIN NUT BREAD

1 ½	cups cooking oil	375 mL
2	cups sugar	500 mL
4	eggs	4
2	cups pumpkin	500 mL
3	cups flour	750 mL
2	teaspoons baking powder	10 mL
2	teaspoons ginger	10 mL
2	teaspoons cloves	10 mL
2	teaspoons nutmeg	10 mL
2	teaspoons cinnamon	10 mL
2	teaspoons soda	10 mL
1	teaspoon salt	5 mL
1	cup walnuts, chopped	250 mL

Mix the oil and sugar until light and fluffy. Add eggs, one at a time, beating well after each addition. Stir in the pumpkin. Sift together dry ingredients. With a few strokes quickly combine the pumpkin mixture, dry ingredients and nuts. Turn into greased loaf pans. Bake at 350°F (180°C) for 1 hour. Yield: 2 loaves

BLUEBERRY COFFEE CAKE

¼	cup shortening	60 mL
¾	cup sugar	175 mL
1	egg	1
1	teaspoon vanilla	5 mL
¾	cup milk	175 mL
1¾	cups flour	425 mL
½	teaspoon salt	2 mL
1	tablespoon baking powder	15 mL
1½	cups blueberries	375 mL
2	tablespoons sugar	30 mL
½	teaspoon cinnamon	2 mL

Beat together shortening, sugar, egg and vanilla until creamy. Add milk and blend well. Mix flour, salt and baking powder, then add to the first mixture, stirring only to moisten. Spread half the batter in a greased 8-inch (20 cm) square pan. Cover with blueberries. Sprinkle with half of the sugar. Cover with remaining batter. Sprinkle with a mixture of sugar and cinnamon. Bake at 375°F (190°C) for 35 to 40 minutes. Yield: 16 servings

GRANOLA-DATE COFFEE CAKE

1	cup dates, chopped	250 mL
½	cup water	125 mL
½	teaspoon vanilla	2 mL
½	cup butter or margarine	125 mL
⅔	cup sugar	150 mL
1	egg	1
1	teaspoon baking powder	5 mL
¼	teaspoon salt	1 mL
1	cup flour	250 mL
⅓	cup granola	75 mL
1	cup brown sugar	250 mL
⅓	cup flour	75 mL
2	tablespoons butter	30 mL

Place dates and water in a small saucepan; cover and simmer 10 minutes. Stir in vanilla. Cool.

Cream butter with sugar; add egg and beat well. Stir in dry ingredients. In another bowl, make topping by mixing granola, brown sugar, ⅓ cup (85 mL) flour and butter.

Spread ¾ of batter in greased 8-inch (20 cm) square pan. Top with date mixture and cover with remainder of batter. Sprinkle with topping. Bake at 350°F (180°C) for 45 minutes. Yield: 16 servings

ROLLED-OAT CAKE

1	cup rolled oats	250 mL
1½	cups boiling water	375 mL
½	cup butter	125 mL
1	cup brown sugar	250 mL
1	teaspoon vanilla	5 mL
1	cup flour	250 mL
1	teaspoon soda	5 mL
½	teaspoon salt	2 mL
1	cup dates, chopped	250 mL
½	cup walnuts, chopped	125 mL

Put rolled oats in bowl and add boiling water. Let stand until cool. Cream butter, add sugar, then beat in rolled oats and vanilla. Sift dry ingredients. Add to first mixture along with dates and nuts; beat and blend well. Bake in 9-inch (22 cm) square pan at 350°F (180°C) for 35 minutes.

GRANOLA-BANANA COOKIES

⅓	cup shortening	100 mL
½	cup sugar	125 mL
¼	cup molasses	50 mL
1	egg	1
1⅓	cups ripe banana, mashed	300 mL
¼	cup skim milk powder	50 mL
1¼	cups flour	300 mL
1	teaspoon baking powder	5 mL
½	teaspoon salt	2 mL
¼	teaspoon baking soda	1 mL
¼	teaspoon ginger	1 mL
½	teaspoon lemon rind, grated	2 mL
½	cup flaked coconut	125 mL
2	tablespoons sesame seeds	30 mL
¾	cup raisins	175 mL
1	cup slow-cooking oats	250 mL

Cream shortening with sugar. Beat in molasses and egg. Stir in banana and milk powder. Sift together flour, baking powder, salt, baking soda and ginger; blend into batter. Stir in lemon rind, coconut, sesame seeds, raisins and oats. Drop by spoonfuls onto greased baking sheet. Bake at 400°F (200°C) for 10 minutes. Yield: 48 cookies

GRANOLA-RAISIN COOKIES

6	tablespoons margarine	90 mL
½	cup brown sugar	125 mL
1	egg, beaten	1
½	teaspoon vanilla	2 mL
3	tablespoons milk	45 mL
¼	teaspoon baking soda	1 mL
2	teaspoons water	10 mL
1	cup flour	250 mL
1	teaspoon baking powder	5 mL
¼	teaspoon salt	1 mL
½	cup raisins	125 mL
1	cup granola	250 mL

Cream margarine with brown sugar. Add egg and vanilla and beat well. Add milk and baking soda dissolved in water; mix. Sift together flour, baking powder and salt; add to batter and beat. Fold in granola and raisins. Drop by spoonfuls onto greased baking sheet. Bake at 375°F (190°C) for 10 to 12 minutes. Yield: 36 cookies

GRANOLA-CHIP COOKIES

6	tablespoons margarine	90 mL
¼	cup brown sugar	50 mL
¼	cup honey	50 mL
1	egg, beaten	1
½	teaspoon vanilla	2 mL
1	cup flour	250 mL
¼	teaspoon salt	1 mL
½	teaspoon baking soda	2 mL
1	cup crunchy honey-almond granola	250 mL
1	6-ounce package chocolate chips	170 g

Cream margarine with sugar and honey. Add egg and vanilla. Sift together dry ingredients and stir in. Fold in granola and chocolate chips. Drop by spoonfuls onto greased baking sheet. Bake at 375°F (190°C) for 8 minutes. Yield: 36 cookies.

HEALTH COOKIES

1	cup margarine	250 mL
1¼	cups brown sugar	300 mL
1	egg	1
2	cups rolled oats	500 mL
1	cup coconut	250 mL
⅓	cup flaked brewer's yeast	75 mL
⅓	cup wheat germ	75 mL
½	teaspoon salt	2 mL
1	cup whole wheat flour	250 mL
2	teaspoons baking powder	10 mL

Cream margarine and sugar. Add egg, beat well until light and fluffy. Add rolled oats, coconut, yeast, wheat germ and salt. Sift flour and baking powder together, and stir to make a soft dough. Drop by spoonfuls onto greased cookie sheet. Bake at 375°F (190°C) for 10 minutes. Yield: 40 cookies

HEALTH RAISIN-OAT COOKIES

½	cup margarine	125 mL
1	cup brown sugar	250 mL
1	egg	1
½	cup peanut butter	125 mL
1	teaspoon vanilla	5 mL
¾	cup whole wheat flour	175 mL
¼	cup wheat germ, toasted	65 mL
½	cup skim milk powder	125 mL
¾	teaspoon salt	3 mL
¼	teaspoon baking powder	1 mL
1	cup quick-cooking rolled oats	250 mL
¼	teaspoon baking soda	1 mL
1	cup raisins	250 mL
	sesame seeds (optional)	

Cream margarine and sugar. Add egg, peanut butter and vanilla and cream until light. Stir in dry ingredients, then add raisins. Drop by spoonfuls onto greased cookie sheet and flatten by hand to form cookies 2 inches (5 cm) in diameter. Sprinkle with sesame seeds if desired. Bake at 375°F (190°C) for 10 minutes. Carefully remove to rack to cool. Yield: 40 cookies

CARROT-OAT COOKIES

½	cup shortening	125 mL
¾	cup sugar	175 mL
½	cup molasses	125 mL
1	egg	1
1	cup carrots, grated	250 mL
¼	cup raisins	65 mL
1¼	cup rolled oats	315 mL
1	cup flour	250 mL
1	teaspoon baking powder	5 mL
½	teaspoon salt	2 mL
¼	teaspoon soda	1 mL
¼	teaspoon nutmeg	1 mL
¼	teaspoon cinnamon	1 mL
¼	cup skim milk powder	65 mL

Cream shortening with sugar. Beat in molasses and egg. Fold in carrots, raisins and rolled oats. Sift flour, baking powder, salt, soda and spices with skim milk powder. Stir into shortening mixture. Drop by spoonfuls onto greased baking sheet. Bake at 375°F (190°C) for 15 minutes. Yield: 60 cookies

OATMEAL COOKIES

½	cup margarine	125 mL
½	cup sugar	125 mL
2	eggs	2
6	tablespoons molasses	90 mL
1¾	cups whole wheat flour	435 mL
1	teaspoon baking powder	5 mL
1	teaspoon cinnamon	5 mL
½	teaspoon salt	2 mL
2	cups rolled oats	500 mL
1	cup raisins	250 mL

Cream margarine and sugar. Add eggs and molasses and beat until light and fluffy. Stir in remainder of ingredients. Drop by spoonfuls onto lightly greased cookie sheet. Bake at 325°F (160°C) for 10 to 12 minutes. Yield: 60 cookies

CARROT-NUT TORTE

6	eggs	6
10	tablespoons honey	150 mL
1	cup carrot, grated	250 mL
1	cup walnuts, chopped	250 mL
1	teaspoon cinnamon	5 mL
½	cup whole wheat flour	125 mL
¼	cup soy flour	65 mL
2	tablespoons rice flour	30 mL
2	tablespoons wheat germ	30 mL

Separate eggs. Beat yolks and honey until light and creamy. Add carrots, walnuts, cinnamon, flours and wheat germ. Beat whites until stiff. Fold into mixture. Pour into greased 8-inch (20 cm) square pan. Bake at 350°F (180°C) for 45 minutes. Yield: 32 bars

WHEAT-GERM APPLE CRISP

4 or 5	apples	4 or 5
1	teaspoon cinnamon	5 mL
1	tablespoon lemon juice	15 mL
½	cup wheat germ	125 mL
½	cup brown sugar	125 mL
¼	cup flour	50 mL
¼	cup butter or margarine	50 mL

Core and slice unpeeled apples into greased 8-inch (20 cm) square baking dish. Sprinkle with cinnamon and lemon juice. Mix wheat germ, brown sugar, flour with butter until crumbly. Put on top of apples. Bake at 350°F (180°C) for 1 hour. Yield: 5 servings

BILL'S PORRIDGE

2½	cups boiling water	625 mL
½	teaspoon salt	2 mL
¾	cup quick-cooking rolled oats	175 mL
½	cup dates, finely chopped	125 mL
½	cup wheat germ	125 mL
½	teaspoon cinnamon	2 mL

Add salt to boiling water. Slowly stir in rolled oats. Then add dates, wheat germ and cinnamon. Simmer 15 minutes. Serve hot. Yield: 4 servings

CRUNCHY GRANOLA

8	cups slow-cooking rolled oats	2 L
2	cups wheat germ	500 mL
½	cup sesame seeds or sunflower seeds	125 mL
1	cup unsweetened coconut	250 mL
1	cup butter or margarine	250 mL
1	cup honey	250 mL
2	tablespoons milk	30 mL
1	tablespoon salt	15 mL

Combine dry ingredients except wheat germ. Add butter or margarine, honey, milk and salt, stirring constantly. Spread on greased baking sheet. Toast at 300°F (150°C) for 20 to 30 minutes until browned, stirring 2 or 3 times during cooking. Add wheat germ 5 minutes before end of cooking time. Cool and store in tightly covered container. Yield: 10 cups (2.5 L)

FRUIT-NUT GRANOLA

1	cup slow-cooking rolled oats	250 mL
1	cup shredded wheat, crushed	250 mL
½	cup unsweetened coconut	125 mL
¼	cup wheat germ	50 mL
½	cup cashews, peanuts or almonds	125 mL
½	cup sunflower seeds	125 mL
4	tablespoons sesame seeds	60 mL
⅓	cup cooking oil	75 mL
1	teaspoon vanilla	5 mL
¼	cup seedless raisins	50 mL
⅓	cup honey	75 mL

Mix dry ingredients. Mix oil, vanilla and honey in a small saucepan; heat until warm. Add to dry ingredients, stirring constantly. Spread on greased baking sheet. Toast at 300°F (150°C) for 25 minutes. Remove from oven. Add raisins while mixture is still warm. Store in glass jar. Yield: 4½ cups (1 L)

OUTDOOR
COOKING

BARBECUE BASICS

Barbecue is a word with several meanings. Originally barbecue meant a feast where animals were roasted whole. Today it usually means a gathering of people cooking meat or fish outdoors, but it might equally refer to a special sauce or a meat dish served on a bun.

Nothing is more appetizing than the sight and aroma of food grilling over glowing coals but only practice brings consistent results. For the novice, the following suggestions will bring greater enjoyment to barbecuing.

THE FIRE

Whatever the food to be cooked, the important thing is a good fire.

Allow 30 to 45 minutes to get a good fire going. A briquet fire can be started with crumpled paper and a few thin sticks but an electric or commercial starter will hurry the process. Drizzle the liquid starter on a pyramid of briquettes, let it stand and then light with a match. Resist the temptation to add more starter. Soon a few coals will show whitish gray. In another 15 to 30 minutes all coals will have a red glow and a covering of gray ash. Only then can you spread them out and start to cook.

Solid and semi-solid starters are available also. Never use kerosene because it gives a flavor. Under no circumstances use gasoline.

CHOOSE THE RIGHT FUEL

Charcoal briquets are the most popular form of fuel, but briquets vary according to their source. The best come from hardwoods. Wood is great too, if it is available, and hardwoods are best for grilling. Resinous woods like pine give a poor flavor.

Don't waste the fuel. Spread it out. If you heap it three briquets deep, it will burn all evening.

When cooking is done, smother or douse the charcoal. It can be dried later and reused.

Remember to use charcoal briquets in a well ventilated place.

STARTING TO COOK

Coals that glow with an even color and smokeless heat are just right. Briquets should have an ash-grey covering over glowing interiors. When all briquets are ready, use tongs to arrange them under the cooking area for grilling or to the rear and the edge for rotisserie cooking. Consult the manual for your equipment.

To test the heat of a fire, place your hand above it at the distance at which food will be cooked, and count slowly until you are forced to pull your hand away from the heat. A count of "one" means a high heat, "three" means medium heat and "five"means low heat.

The experienced chef adjusts the grill or fire box or moves food items away from or toward, the center of the fire. If the fire is right, leave it alone. Add new fuel at the edge when necessary.

Once the fire is under way, disturb it as little as possible. Constant poking lowers the temperature. Knocking grey ash off briquets will raise the temperature.

BEYOND CONTROL

Temperature and humidity, direction of the wind all influence the fire. If a grill has no hood, a strip of tin rigged to the side will help.

Food should be at room temperature. On cool evenings a longer cooking time is required. Water pistols knock out unwanted flare-ups that give meat a taste of burned fat.

TOOLS

The equipment you must have includes: two pairs of long handled tongs, one for coals and one for meat, a barbecue baster, though a good paintbrush will do, long handled hinged grids that compensate for lack of an adjustable grill, and aluminum foil that takes the place of cooking pots.

ALL DONE — READY TO START AGAIN

Clean the grill after every cookout. The grill, if it was lightly greased, will probably wipe clean with a newspaper or damp cloth. For greater ease, line the grill with heavy duty aluminum foil, shiny side up, to protect the firebox and allow for neat handling of ash. Dry gravel over the foil will help soak up dripping fat. Be sure the gravel is dry and replace it after a few grillings.

BARBECUED GARLIC BREAD

1   Crusty French loaf
                soft butter or margarine
                garlic salt & chopped chives

Cut loaf into thick slices. Spread butter generously on both sides of each slice. Sprinkle garlic salt and chopped chives over butter. Rearrange slices back into loaf form. Wrap with foil. Set on grill, turning occasionally, for 10-15 minutes over medium coals. Yield: 20 slices

BARBECUED 'EGG IN A HOLE'

Make required number of cheese and other types of sandwiches. Cut a 2½ inch circle out of each sandwich. Place on well–greased hot cookie sheet on barbecue grill. Break an egg into each hole. Cook circles and egg filled sandwiches until toasted on underside. Turn and continue cooking until bread is brown and egg cooked. Serve with catsup or chili sauce and a salad.

Plain bread may be used instead of sandwiches.

BARBECUED STEAK

2	pounds round steak	1 kg
¼	cup cooking oil	65 mL
½	cup lemon juice	125 mL
½	cup onion, chopped	125 mL
½	teaspoon celery salt	2 mL
½	teaspoon thyme	2 mL
½	teaspoon rosemary	2 mL
½	teaspoon salt	2 mL
½	teaspoon pepper	2 mL
½	teaspoon oregano	2 mL
1	clove garlic, minced	1

Combine ingredients. Place steak in shallow dish. Pour over marinade.

Cover and refrigerate over night. Turn occasionally. Place well–drained steak over hot coals. Cook to desired doneness.

BARBECUED ROUND STEAK ROAST

Have the butcher remove the bone, roll and tie a 6 to 10 pound round steak roast (3-5 kg).

Insert the spit and fasten clamps so that roast is evenly balanced. Coat the roast with the following mixture:

½	cup margarine	125 g
2	teaspoons dry mustard	10 mL
½	teaspoon garlic powder	2 mL
¼	teaspoon horseradish powder	1 mL
1	teaspoon Worcestershire sauce	5 mL
½	teaspoon salt	2 mL

Place roast over a hot bed of coals with the spit fitted into the electric motor mount; rotate the roast for approximately four hours or until done. Reduce cooking time for medium or rare roast.

BARBECUED MOOSE STEAK

2	steaks	2
½	cup oil	125 mL
¼	cup vinegar	65 mL
2	cloves garlic, crushed	2
1	teaspoon salt	5 mL
1	tablespoon parsley, chopped	15 mL
½	teaspoon oregano	2 mL
¼	teaspoon thyme	1 mL

Trim fat from steaks. Place in shallow dish. Make marinade by combining remainder of ingredients in a jar, shake well.

Pour marinade over steak, cover and refrigerate over night; turn occasionally. Place well-drained steaks on barbecue grill. Cook 10 minutes per side.

BARBECUED BOLOGNA

4	pounds bologna	2 kg
	whole cloves	
1	cup brown sugar	250 mL
2	tablespoons prepared mustard	30 mL
3	tablespoons vinegar	45 mL
1	teaspoon grated orange rind	5 mL

Remove plastic casing from bologna. Score in diamond shape, stud with cloves. Insert spit lengthwise in bologna, lock in place with prongs. Cook over medium-to-low heat for 30 minutes.

Combine remaining ingredients. Baste bologna every 10 to 15 minutes for 30 minutes more, using all the sauce. Yield: 12 servings

BARBECUED HAMBURGERS

1½	pounds ground beef	.75 kg
2	eggs beaten	2
½	cup onion, chopped	125 mL
2	tablespoons milk	30 mL
2	teaspoons Worcestershire sauce	10 mL
1	teaspoon salt	5 mL
¼	teaspoon pepper	1 mL
¼	cup catsup	65 mL
2	teaspoons horseradish	15 mL

In a large bowl mix beef, egg, onion and seasonings. Shape into six large patties. Cook on grill 5 inches (12 cm) from coals. Cook 5 minutes per side for medium, cook 8 minutes per side for well-done hamburgers. Yield: 6 large hamburgers.

BARBECUED MEAT LOAVES

2	eggs, beaten	2
2	pounds ground beef	1 kg
2	cups soft bread crumbs	500 mL
¾	cup onion, minced	175 mL
2	tablespoons horseradish	30 mL
2	teaspoons salt	10 mL
1	teaspoon dry mustard	5 mL
¼	cup milk	65 mL
½	cup margarine	125 mL
½	cup catsup	125 mL

Mix eggs with meat, bread crumbs and onion. Add horseradish, salt and mustard; blend in milk. Shape into 5 small meat loaves. Place in wire basket. Melt margarine, add catsup. Brush over all sides of loaves. Cook loaves over slow coals for 20 minutes; turn and brush all sides with sauce. Cook 15 minutes more. Serve with remainder of sauce. Yield: 5 generous servings

BARBECUE CHICKEN

1	fryer chicken	1
¼	cup honey	50 mL
¼	cup lemon juice	50 mL
¼	cup butter	50 mL
¼	cup apricot nectar	50 mL

Cut chickens in pieces. Place chicken skin-side up on grill, about 4 inches (10 cm) above coals. Place all ingredients in a saucepan, bring to the boil. Baste chicken frequently with sauce. Cook for about 1 hour, turning pieces every 15 minutes.

BARBECUED CHICKEN IN SAUCE

1	fryer chicken	1
1	cup catsup	250 mL
½	cup onion, chopped	125 mL
3	tablespoons Worcestershire sauce	45 mL
¼	cup vinegar	50 mL
3	tablespoons sugar	45 mL
2	teaspoons dry mustard	10 mL
¼	teaspoon pepper	1 mL

To prepare the sauce, combine catsup, onion, Worcestershire sauce and vinegar; add sugar, mustard and pepper. Simmer 15 minutes.

Cut chicken in pieces. Arrange individual portions of chicken on two squares of aluminum foil. Pour sauce over the chicken pieces. Bring foil up over food and seal edges to make a tight package. Place on the grill over fire, cook 2 hours, turning packages occasionally.

BARBECUED PORK CHOPS

6	loin chops	6
¾	cup cooking oil	175 mL
¼	cup soya sauce	50 mL
½	cup cider vinegar	125 mL
2	tablespoons Worcestershire sauce	30 mL
1	teaspoon dry mustard	5 mL
1	teaspoon sage	5 mL
1	teaspoon salt	5 mL
½	teaspoon black pepper	2 mL
1	clove garlic, crushed	1

Use chops 1 inch (2.5 cm) thick; snip edges of chops to prevent curling. Place in shallow dish. Make marinade by combining remainder of ingredients in a jar, shake well.

Pour marinade over chops, cover and refrigerate overnight. Turn occasionally. Place well-drained chops on grill 5 inches (12.5 cm) from coals and cook slowly, 20 to 25 minutes each side. Heat marinade in small pan, brush chops frequently with marinade during cooking. Yield: 6 servings

137

BARBECUED SPARERIBS

4-6	pounds spareribs	2-3 kg

Ribs can be grilled from start to finish over coals, but you can shorten cooking time by pre-cooking ribs. Simmer ribs in water for an hour; drain and pat dry. Place pre-cooked spareribs on barbecue grill about 4 inches (10 cm) above slow coals. Cook 10 minutes on each side, basting frequently with one of the following sauces:

HONEY AND LEMON SAUCE

½	cup cooking oil	125 mL
6	tablespoons honey	90 mL
2	teaspoons lemon juice	10 mL
¼	teaspoon garlic salt	1 mL
¼	teaspoon dry mustard	1 mL
¼	teaspoon Tabasco sauce	1 mL

Combine all ingredients and simmer 10 minutes.

ONION SAUCE

¼	cup oil	65 mL
1½	cups water	375 mL
1	package onion-soup mix	42 g

Combine all ingredients and simmer 10 minutes.

HOT BARBECUE SAUCE

¼	cup butter	50 mL
¾	cup onion, chopped	185 mL
¼	cup brown sugar	50 mL
1	clove garlic, crushed	1
2	teaspoons salt	10 mL
2	teaspoons chili powder	10 mL
1	teaspoon dry mustard	5 mL
1	cup pineapple juice	250 mL
1	cup catsup	250 mL
½	cup lime juice	125 mL
½	cup chili sauce	125 mL
1	tablespoon soya sauce	15 mL
¼	teaspoon Tabasco sauce	1 mL

Combine all ingredients and simmer 30 minutes.

ZESTY FILLET BARBECUE

2	pounds fresh fish fillets	1 kg
¼	cup chili sauce	65 mL
2	tablespoons cooking oil	30 mL
2	tablespoons prepared mustard	30 mL
2	tablespoons onion, grated	30 mL
1	tablespoon lemon juice	15 mL
1	teaspoon salt	5 mL
1	teaspoon Worcestershire sauce	5 mL
¼	teaspoon pepper	1 mL

Cut fillets into serving-sized portions. Combine remaining ingredients, mix thoroughly. Coat fillets with sauce. Place in well-greased, hinged wire grills. Cook about 4 inches (10 cm) above moderately hot coals for 5 to 8 minutes time; depending on thickness.

Baste with sauce; turn and cook 5 to 8 minutes longer, or until fish flakes easily when tested with a fork. Yield: 6 servings

FISH CAKES

1	cup cooked fish	250 mL
2	cups mashed potato	500 mL
1	egg, beaten	1
1	teaspoon salt	5 mL
¼	teaspoon pepper	1 mL

Toss all ingredients together lightly. Shape into patties. Place on well-greased, hinged wire grill. Cook over hot coals until brown on both sides. Yield: 6 servings

HOT TUNA BURGERS

1	7-ounce can tuna	198 g
½	cup cheddar cheese, shredded	125 mL
1	cup celery, chopped	250 mL
¼	teaspoon salt	1 mL
¼	teaspoon pepper	1 mL
¼	cup mayonnaise	50 mL
2	tablespoons catsup	30 mL
1	teaspoon lemon juice	5 mL
4	hamburger buns	4

Set buns aside. Combine remaining ingredients. Chill thoroughly until cooking time.

Spoon mixture into sliced buns, wrap each bun in aluminum foil, heat over glowing charcoal for 15 minutes, turning frequently. Yield: 4 servings.

CUBS COOK-OUT MEAL

2	pounds ground beef	1 kg
½	cup onion, diced	125 mL
¼	cup pepper, minced	65 mL
2	teaspoons salt	10 mL
3	7½-ounce cans tomato sauce	639 mL
1	19-ounce can beans with pork	540 mL

Brown ground beef, add onions and green pepper. Add salt, tomato sauce and beans. Simmer a few minutes. Serve on buns or over baked potatoes. Yield: 8 servings

FOOD IN FOIL

Arrange individual portions of prepared food on squares of heavy-duty aluminum foil. Add salt, pepper and one tablespoon (15 mL) butter. Bring foil up over food and seal all edges with double folds to make a tight package. Place on the grill and turn frequently. Try opening a package to find out if food is cooked before summoning the family.

POTATOES ANNA

Arrange potato slices, add grated cheese and onion soup mix; cook 30 minutes.

POTATOES

Arrange potato slices; cook 1 hour.

GLAZED CARROTS

Arrange cooked carrots and add dash mustard, sprinkle corn syrup and nutmeg; cook 15 minutes.

BEEF PATTIES

Arrange beef patties with carrot sticks, onion slices, tomato slices and sprinkle with brown gravy mix; cook for 1 hour.

CHICKEN DINNER

Arrange chicken pieces with potato slices, tomato slices, onion slices, mushrooms and green pepper rings; sprinkle with Worcestershire sauce and paprika; cook 1¼ hours.

SWISS STEAK

Arrange individual portions of steak with carrot sticks, onions quartered, potato strips, pepper rings, chopped celery and sprinkle with catsup; cook 40 minutes.

PORK CHOPS

Arrange marinated pork chops with apple rings; cook 45 minutes.

FRANKLY SKY SKRAPERS

Arrange buns, split wieners, beans, chopped onions, cheese slice; sprinkle with mustard and celery seeds; cook 15 minutes.

FISH

Arrange fillets with pepper slices, onion slices; cook 10 minutes.

BANANAS

Arrange bananas with brown sugar and lemon juice; cook 15 minutes. Garnish with red jelly and shredded coconut.

PEACHES

Arrange canned or fresh peach halves and fill with mincemeat; cook 20 minutes on edge of grill.

BARBECUE SAUCE

2	cups tomato juice	500 mL
1	package onion-soup mix	42 g
½	cup catsup	125 mL
¼	cup vinegar	50 mL
2	teaspoons Worcestershire sauce	10 mL
2	tablespoons sugar	30 mL
½	teaspoon salt	2 mL
¼	teaspoon pepper	1 mL

Mix all ingredients together and simmer for 15 minutes. Apply sauce to meat near the end of cooking time.

FOUR-SEASON BARBECUE SAUCE

½	cup margarine	125 mL
½	cup chopped onions	125 mL
⅓	cup syrup	75 mL
1	tablespoon Worcestershire sauce	15 mL
1	teaspoon dry mustard	5 mL
½	cup vinegar	125 mL
1	cup tomato juice	250 mL
1	cup catsup	250 mL
1	teaspoon salt	5 mL
1	teaspoon paprika	5 mL

Melt margarine, add onions and remainder of ingredients. Bring to boil and simmer 15 to 20 minutes. Apply sauce to meat near the end of the cooking time.

SWEET AND SOUR BARBECUE SAUCE

2	tablespoons cornstarch	30 mL
½	cup water	125 mL
¼	cup brown sugar	65 mL
¼	cup vinegar	65 mL
¼	cup catsup	65 mL
1	tablespoon soya sauce	15 mL

Dissolve corn starch in water. Add remaining ingredients and simmer 10 minutes. Apply sauce to steak or hamburger near the end of cooking time.

MELTING MOMENTS

Delicious, enjoyed by young and old.

12	marshmallows	12
12	graham wafers	12
12	squares milk chocolate	12

Toast two marshmallows until brown. Place on wafer. Top with two squares of milk chocolate. Cover with another wafer — sandwich style. Eat immediately. Yield: 6 sandwich cookies.

DOUGH BOYS

2	cups flour	500 mL
4½	teaspoons baking powder	25 mL
½	teaspoon salt	2 mL
3	tablespoons shortening	45 mL
⅞	cup milk	220 mL

Mix and sift dry ingredients. With 2 knives or pastry blender, cut in shortening. Add milk and mix with a fork to form a soft dough.

Peel a stick three inches (8 cm) down from top; grease stick. Wrap biscuit dough around the peeled stick and bake slowly over the coals. Turn stick so dough cooks evenly. When the dough is baked it pulls off the stick easily. Fill the hole with butter and jam.

INDEX

C

D

E

F

G